THE YOKE OF DIVINE LOVE

DOM HUBERT VAN ZELLER

THE YOKE OF DIVINE LOVE

A study of conventual perfection

THE CENACLE PRESS
AT SILVERSTREAM PRIORY

This edition is based upon the second impression printed
in 1958 of *The Yoke of Divine Love: A Study of Conventual Perfection*
published by Burns Oates & Washbourne Ltd.

This edition republished 2025 by Silverstream Priory
with the kind permission of Downside Abbey.
New material and graphic design copyright
© 2025 by Silverstream Priory.

All rights reserved:
No part of this book may be reproduced or transmitted,
in any form or by any means, without permission.

The Cenacle Press at Silverstream Priory
Silverstream Priory
Stamullen, County Meath, K32 T189, Ireland
www.cenaclepress.com

Nihil Obstat: Dom A.M. Young, OSB
Censor Congreg. Angliae OSB
Imprimatur: H.K. Byrne, OSB
Ab. Praes.
20 June 1956

Nihil Obstat: Hubertus Richards, STL, LSS
Censor Deputatus
Imprimatur: + Georgius L. Craven
Episcopus Sebastopolis
Vic. Cap. Westmon.
Westmonasterii: 31 December 1956

ISBN 978-1-915544-15-5

Book and cover design by Enrique J. Aguilar

PREFACE

THE subtitle needs a word of explanation. 'How', it might be asked, 'can conventual perfection differ from any other kind of Christian perfection? How can monasticism bring anything new to perfection? Christ preaches counsels of perfection which monks and nuns aim at fulfilling. A great number of lay people also aim at fulfilling them. Christian perfection means living Christ's life and Christ did not lead two lives—one to be followed in the world and one to be followed in the cloister—but a single life to be followed by everybody.' To this it might be answered that Christ lives as many lives as there are created souls, each soul finding in his own life the life of Christ. But apart from such an answer, which might appear fanciful to some, there is the evidence of the counsels themselves. Unless the words 'If you will be perfect, go and sell what you possess' have been misapplied for centuries, they refer to the religious vocation, and only in a more general way to the renunciation made by those who, while living in the world, practise poverty, chastity, and obedience on their own.

The difference between a soul striving after holiness in the world and one doing the same thing in a monastery may not be great. The efforts made and means taken are relative to the given opportunity. There can be no absolute system of measurement: the whole thing depends upon the response to the respective grace. If the grace is appropriate, the response is appropriate—and therefore different. So it is more than merely a question of degree in respective responsibilities; it is a question of the kind of standard set. Spirituality is spirituality whatever you are, but the nature of conventual perfection is different from the nature of secular perfection—just as the nature of eremitic perfection is different from either.

The manner of conforming to the pattern of Christ will in this book be taken as the monastic manner. Religious must find Christ in their submission, in their prayer, in their community life. To the extent that they seriously attempt this they are true religious; to the extent that they do not they are false. It is as simple as that. Failure in vocation is nothing else than letting go of the life of Christ; success is nothing else than living it.

Another point to be noted is that no attempt will be made in this study to review the historical development of the conventual tradition. Still less to examine the theological implications contained in its spirituality. The present purpose is rather to present the ideal which has been partly the inspiration and partly the outcome of monastic tradition and theology. The ideas expressed will be shown to have precedent in the orthodox past, but it is not for the sake of the past that they are expressed. From St Benedict's time to our own the monastic life has rested on certain fundamentals—prayer, reading, silence, labour, enclosure—and the whole question for the individual religious is how to work upward from these to God and not inwards towards self. This is the whole of monastic spirituality and the whole concern of this book. We are not so much interested in how our fathers managed it as how, in the setting of our lives, we are to manage it.

There have been different schools of spirituality in the past, and in spite of the standardized age in which we live there are different schools of spirituality today, but when you examine what monasticism precisely stands for you can get down to something very near to a formula. A synthesis is aimed at here, and if one or other aspect of religious perfection is given more than its measure of attention it is only because that particular aspect is felt to have been neglected.

If Benedictine saints and writers are those most drawn upon, it is because those who take the Benedictine vows are mostly envisaged as readers. The subject matter, however, is not restricted to the Benedictine tradition, and certainly there is no Benedictine axe to grind. Avoiding all controversy for the snare that it is, we can nevertheless trace in the history of monasticism a variety of trends which, in thirteen centuries of experiment, have developed out of a common doctrine. Racial and cultural influences have played their part, reforms of one sort or another have given to its polity, and even to its spirituality, new directions; particular needs of the Church have occasioned new forms of expression. But always the common monastic ideal has held the movement together and kept it on the move. Even if homogeneity has not always been secured, at least the enterprise has always been alive. Factors which for a time looked as though they were killing the original conception of the life have, when either their first energy has spent itself or when some counterbalancing interest has come along, revealed themselves in the long view as constructive and life-giving. Exaggeration is often a sign of vitality, and monasticism is both big enough and vigorous enough to be able to assimilate sideline excesses. The claims, legitimate in themselves but liable to be expressed at the expense of the life as a whole, which in one epoch or another have been made by scholarship, education, pastoral work or the solitary vocation, have been found in the end to emphasize the basic principles rather than to overlay them or substitute new ones. In the religious life there can be no substitute for prayer and withdrawal from the world. It is as if each new interpretation of monasticism, springing up as a stream on the side of a mountain, draws attention to the main current which has its origin far back in the valley: each is swallowed up and the main course flows on. It is the spirituality of this essential monasticism that we intend in this book to consider.

CONTENTS

Preface vii

Book I
The Yoke of the Religious Life

1. Supernatural Motive 3
2. Purpose and Means 11
3. Unworldliness 23
4. Poverty 31
5. Chastity 39
6. Exterior Penance 47
7. Interior Penance 57
8. Obedience 69

Book II
The Yoke of Prayer

1. Individual Prayer 85
2. Liturgical Prayer 95
3. Contemplative Prayer 105
4. Recollection 117
5. The Means 125
6. The Safeguards 137
7. Effects 147

BOOK III
THE YOKE OF COMMUNITY LIFE

1. Common Aim 157
2. Common Principle 165
3. Common Performance 173
4. Common Misconceptions 183
5. Common Progress 197
6. Common Perfection 209

BOOK I
THE YOKE OF THE RELIGIOUS LIFE

1

SUPERNATURAL MOTIVE

THE service of religion stands or falls by its impulse and direction. Unless love is its inspiration it has little to commend it. It will be on the quality of his love that the religious will be judged.

Love alone gives its character to obedience, and obedience in its turn tests the character of love. Without love, obedience can be laziness, orderliness, desire to please, vanity. Given love, every act of obedience is an act of worship.

The problem of religious service is how to make it truly an activity of love. Unless it is interior and supernatural, life under the vows of religion is not more nor less a life of worship than life under the vows of marriage.

The man who loves God in his marriage is obviously giving more glory to God than the religious who loves something other than God in the service of his vows. The religious must keep his vows, not because he loves his vows, but because he loves God.

The religious must keep his vows because God wants his service of love. It is not enough to keep vows for fear of denying to God the service of love. Nor would it, over the whole course of a religious career, be possible to do so.

If we think of religious obedience more as the ban on certain things than as the summons to certain things—particularly to love—we have not learned much of the virtue. The religious vocation is nothing else than the call of divine love to respond with divine love.

St Peter urges us in his first epistle to 'purify our souls in the obedience of charity'.[1] He might equally have urged us to do so in the charity of obedience. If religious service is rightly understood, the terms are interchangeable.

It is our mistake that we think of religious service too much as submission to the rules which govern it, and not enough as the purpose for which it exists. The rules are a caretaker government; the supreme authority is love.

It is our mistake that we spend more of our time examining how we have responded to rule than how we have responded to God. If God were the end of our whole endeavour we would spend little time on examination.

It is our mistake that we let ourselves become more and more dependent upon means and methods, less and less dependent upon God. We can come to keep rules as we would keep pets: to give us a sense of comfort. As pets can be a substitute for people, so rules can be a substitute for God.

Most of us obey rules in the general belief that the letter is safeguarding the spirit. It should do, but there is no absolute guarantee. We know from Scripture that the letter can as easily kill the spirit as quicken it.

We honour rules in the general belief that they are byproducts of the love of God. They should be, but there is no absolute guarantee. Experience shows that they can be parasites as much as offshoots.

Rules are meant to be obeyed, not worshipped. They are designed for our use, for our greater liberty; they are not meant to tie us up in knots. We are subject to rule because we are subject to God.

God is the authority; the rule is the channel of His will. We observe rules, and so dispose ourselves towards God. We do not observe them so as to dispose ourselves towards more rules.

We have to be obedient to legislation because the love of God commands it. It is not a case of having to love God because a law commands it.

Although the first commandment enjoins the love of God, there

---

1   1 Peter 1:22

has to be a readiness to love before the commandment can be obeyed. And the readiness to love is already love.

Law is to be respected, and even loved, in that it expresses the mind of God. God's law represents His will, and His will is as much Himself as His Sacred Heart, so we are clearly right in respecting and loving the law of God.

The only thing is that God must be seen in His law. The law may not be seen so large on the horizon as to block out the vision of God. Man is apt to magnify the law and forget about the mind of the Lawgiver.

Man is apt to invent a whole lot of laws of his own and bow down in worship before them. When this happens, the whole point of the law is lost sight of. God is lost sight of.

Where laws are multiplied you get legalism instead of love. You get system instead of service. You get religiosity instead of religion. It was from such an anomaly that the temple priesthood was suffering in the time of our Lord. The religious life in every age is prone to the same evil.

Where the law is either misconceived, misapplied or misdirected, it runs contrary to the purpose of God. It is not merely waste material, it is bad material. Instead of enlarging, it narrows. Instead of generating love, it embitters.

It is as though the law were able to say to man: 'By making me an end in itself, you have caused me to be false to my nature. You have taken me out of my condition and station. I will revenge myself upon you by making you my slave. Henceforth you will not see God in me; you will see only me.' This is called the curse of the religious life.

Rightly understood, the religious life should be proof against such an inversion. A vocation carries with it the grace to go all the way in love. Only where self remains unrenounced can the letter take over from the spirit and impose a slavery.

Where charity and humility exist together in the soul, there can be no danger that the substance of the religious life will be missed. Charity aims at communicating itself to everything—and consequently to the observance of the law—while humility subjects itself primarily to the spirit of the law—which is ultimately the Spirit of God—and therefore finds no difficulty in observing the letter according to God.

Without charity and humility the religious life would be meaningless. It would also be much harder than it is. Then indeed would the yoke be heavy and bitter. But because men take up the burden in charity, and bear the yoke in voluntary subjection with Christ, the religious life holds the promise of happiness as well as holiness.

Isaias's attack upon the religious life of his period exposes the fatal tendency of those dedicated to the service of God. 'In the day of your fast your own will is found ... is this such a fast as I have chosen?'[2]

If we fast for the love of fasting and not for the love of God, what is there to choose between fasting and feasting? If we sacrifice to God because we like the idea of sacrifice, or the ceremony of sacrifice, or the reputation which our sacrifice gains us, we do not sacrifice to God but to self.

'Offer sacrifice no more in vain,' says Isaias, 'incense is an abomination to me. The new moons and sabbaths and other festivals I will not abide ... my soul hateth your new moons and your solemnities; they are become troublesome to me, and l am weary of bearing them.'[3] What have been lacking are charity and humility.

It is only the humble religious who can accept the doctrine that sacrifice is less important than obedience; only the charitable religious who can make the sacrifice of sacrifice lovingly.

A distinction must be made, then, between obedience and observance. And obedience must be preferred every time.

Obedience goes on as a virtue when observance ceases as an exercise. Obedience is a religious habit, observance a religious practice. Thus the will of a superior dispensing from observance does more towards the subject's sanctification than the observance could do, however lovingly performed.

It is not for the subject to separate observance of the rule from the superior's interpretation of the rule. All the subject has to do is to follow the will of the superior. This is the obediential sacrifice that is greater than other sacrifices—greater than the sacrifices of choice.

Sacrifice in the name of obedience is harder than sacrifice in the

---

[2] Isaias 58:5-6
[3] Isaias 1:13

name of penance. Certainly, it is harder than sacrifice in the name of love. But it is an act of love nevertheless.

In the assent which one man gives to the will of another there must be the desire to see the supernatural in the natural command. The desire need not be expressed, but it must be there. Otherwise, the obedience is purely natural, and neither charity nor humility come into it.

When the material thing commanded runs contrary to the spiritual thing desired, there is a conflict which calls for the exercise of faith. It is now that all the virtues of the soul must rise to the summons of obedience.

When authority abrogates what has been taken to be the will of God, it is not easy to see the will of God in authority. In such a case it must be assumed in faith that God's consequent will is overriding His antecedent will. The general is being waived in favour of the particular and immediate.

It is not for the subject to distinguish between the law and legitimate application of the law. Ultimately the authority is the same. Since the object of obedience is the will of God, the whole question is to determine which aspect of the will of God is the most immediate to the soul. Nothing can be more direct than the signified will of a superior.

The purpose of the law and the purpose of the dispensation from the law are ultimately the same. To see this and accept it is to act supernaturally; to refuse it is to miss the virtue of obedience altogether.

To abide by the law, refusing to be dispensed when it is the will of authority to dispense, is to abide by self and to turn down the claims of humility and love.

There can be no love in a tenacious clinging to a law from which authority has withdrawn. There can be no humility in submitting to a system which is recognized only by self.

'Nor is there any love', the meticulous observer of the law might object, 'in submitting to an authority that dispenses from the observances of love. And where is the humility in acting on the suppression of the exercises that were designed to keep one humble?'

To this it must be answered that obedience is the one sure guarantee of love. The sense of love is no sure guarantee of love. How can we be said to love if we do not the things that are commanded us by those who hold the place of Christ?

And it is the same with humility. Neither to feel humble nor even to do the works of humility is to have the virtue of humility. Humility is subjecting oneself to the will of God. How can we be said to have humility if we refuse to submit ourselves to the will of those who hold the place of Christ?

The religious life is nothing else than the surrender of self in union with the surrender of Christ to His Father's will. If the Father's will demands the elimination of just those things that had stood for the Father's will, then surrender to the Father's will as expressed *now* is the only true surrender.

Once the old forms are empty it is no good hanging on to them. It is like filing envelopes. It is like painting chickens on empty eggshells. The old has to be replaced by the new. New wine must be put in new wine-skins—however much we think the old to be better.

So long as the human will sincerely searches for the divine will and is ready to see the divine will expressed in the will of a superior, nothing can go wrong in the religious life. It is when the subject thinks that he can interpret the divine will better than the superior that things go wrong in the religious life.

The whole secret of the religious life is to will only what God wants. This sounds obvious, but it is a factor easily lost sight of. It is the basic truth on which everything else—observance, work, prayer, human relations, penance and suffering—will be found to rest.

It is not always easy to judge how far we love God's will, love our particular vocation, love God Himself. It is always possible to tell whether or not we will God's will. And if we do, it is counted to us for love. Yes, if we will to follow the will of God, we have no cause to question ourselves about either the love we owe to God or our attitude towards the vocation which He has given us.

'Our desires make us,' says St Augustine; 'we are what we will.' Our feelings do not make us; nor do our theories. We are not what we wish we were, or what we imagine ourselves to be. It is all a matter of the will.

So, if as religious we will to lead the religious life in the terms laid down by God, we are true religious. To desire God's will is to possess it. But there can be a good deal of humbug about this: we can deceive ourselves: we can think we are wanting God's will when we are wanting nothing but self.

In the same way to desire to pray is already to practise prayer. But there can be a good deal of humbug about this too: we can think we are wanting to pray when in fact we are wanting to think of ourselves as praying.

In the same way to desire to love our neighbour is already to possess charity. But even here there can be humbug: we can think we are wanting to be kind when what we really want is to be thought kind, or to feel kind, or to have arrived at a degree of kindness.

So we must be sure that the will is a genuine volition and has God as its object. Otherwise we are back again at self. In order to be a true religious, I must avoid going round in circles with myself as pivot. I must see that my whole desire is something outside myself—namely God. Then shall I be what God means me to be. My desires will be in order, and I shall be what I will.

A vocation is a grace. For just so long as I cooperate with the grace as a grace, it remains something supernatural. If I treat it as a career, it becomes a career. A religious career can, like any other career, be successful. If my career has prospered, and if I have not handled it supernaturally, I shall have had my reward when I come to die.

But the whole point of a vocation is that it has come from God and must go back to God. 'My word shall not return to me void,' saith the Lord.[4] The chances are that if I follow my religious vocation in the spirit of one who has no thought beyond the secular character of his occupation in life, I shall not only make void the word of God's call but also do harm in the world.

It is of vital importance, then, that the direction of religious effort be kept single and supernatural. Of themselves the exercises of the religious life do not secure this. They help the soul along—if the soul is prepared to use them rightly—but they do not carry the soul all the

---

4   Isaias 55:11

way. They are as oars to the rower. The rower still has need to steer and to pull.

The effects of routine, weariness, absorbing work, counter attractions and the sense of having earned a rest are liable to render the soul indifferent to the supernatural motive. That one's life is set towards God is taken for granted. But one's life has constantly to be reset; nothing may be taken for granted.

Religious life, like married life, begins again every day. Religious life, like married life, is the life of love. And love never stops still.

The expression of any kind of life which is founded on love is inevitably that of sacrifice. Love of God, love of a person, love of an ideal: each involves immolation. The terms of love are unconditional surrender constantly repeated.

The religious life is not consummated in the single act of pronouncing vows. Religious profession confirms the sacrifice; it does not conclude it. In a sense it begins it.

Like the burning shrub which Moses saw in the desert, the sacrifice of the monk is one which goes on all the time and which never seems to reach its climax. Or rather it is always at its climax. There is no consuming, since true love knows no falling away.

Selfless, unremitting, relying upon the grace of God and not upon human strength, the will of the monk is *in via perfectionis*.[5] But it is always in the power of the monk to lower the will, to re-direct his purpose, to forget what he came into religion for. 'In every work of thine,' says Ecclesiasticus, 'regard thy soul in faith; for this is the keeping of the commandments.'[6]

---

5   In the way of perfection.
6   Ecclesiasticus 32:27

2

PURPOSE AND MEANS

WHETHER the immediate or the ultimate end of the religious life is considered, the result is the same. To give glory to God is the object both of the present act and the remote purpose. You might say that Christ is at once the purpose and the means. 'The foundation which has been laid is the only one which anyone can lay; I mean Jesus Christ.'[1] The religious life begins and ends with Christ. There can be no Christian monasticism apart from Him.

When we examine the practical aspect of this proposition, we have to narrow the field. While the remote end of the religious life remains always charity, union with God, reliving the life of Christ, the proximate end is to provide an environment which furthers this charity, union, and Christlife. Every detail of the external life is designed to foster the life of the spirit, is planned towards creating that atmosphere in which the love of God and neighbour is most likely to develop.

So the religious life is essentially constructive, liberative, positive. The monastic vocation is not primarily a call to flee the world; it is primarily a call to union with God. But where all Christians are called to union with God through Christ, the religious is called to union with God through Christ in a particular setting.

---

[1] 1 Corinthians 3:11

The monastic life involves flight from the world but supposes search. Flight would be no good without search. It is the function of the particular religious order to construct, and to keep in repair, the framework wherein individual souls may conduct their search.

Early in his Rule, St Benedict gives a positive and a negative view of the work to be performed in monasteries of his observance: '*Deum quaerere*' is the primary purpose; '*voluntatem proprium deserentes*' shows the way it may be done.[2]

All that a founder or monastic legislator can do is to offer a system which points to perfection. His aim is to free his subjects from the weights which would normally act as a drag on spiritual progress. And, having freed them, to indicate the way of perfection.

The Rule does not so much impose burdens which sanctify as strike off chains which do not. The trouble is that monks can live with their faces so close to the anvil that the very strokes which are calculated to make them free are taken only as part of the slavery.

Every duty, every correction, every community exercise, every bell should proclaim the positive character of the religious life; each is a summons to the service of love. Every movement of a man's vocation is meant to be a witness to the life of Christ.

'What says any man when he speaks of Thee?' St Augustine asks. 'Yet woe to him that does not speak.' The same might be applied to the various activities of the monastic life. Our observances amount to precious little in our interpretation of Christ's life; yet woe to us if we are not observant.

It is in and through our observances that we find our way to Christ. It is in and through Christ that our observances have any value. The required conformity is that of our wills to Christ's. It is a personal and supernatural act. We do not conform for the sake of conformity.

To be regular for the sake of regularity, punctual for the sake of punctuality, modest in bearing for the sake of modesty in bearing is to stop short at the most important part. You might just as well be edifying for the sake of edification or be silent for the sake of silence. There is no particular virtue where there is nothing particularly supernatural.

---

2 'To seek God' and 'abandoning one's own will'.

Unless from the outset the religious realizes that nothing about his vocation is of value unless it leads to God, he will find himself getting stuck in the exterior of monasticism and will never come to discover what the thing really stands for. Those elements just mentioned—regularity, humility in movement, silence—are of use to the monk only in the measure that they make for recollection and are observed in virtue of obedience.

Legalism, formalism, ritualism: these things come up in religion, and spoil it, only where the external has become the enemy of the internal. If the outward were always made to take second place it would minister to charity and not offend against it.

Because of man's tendency to set greater store by the spectacle than by the substance, performance of the liturgy can war against liturgical prayer, custody of the eyes can war against the presence of God, ceremony can war against sacrifice.

Man can be so ruled by signs as to be indifferent to their significance, so dictated to by slogans as to be deaf to the Word.

If love does not transcend the symbol, it will be cramped by the symbol. The pastoral staff can be to the monk what the sword is to the Moslem. The cross itself loses its significance if the mind does not move on to the Crucified.

Moses, when he saw that it was becoming an object of superstition and was no longer raising the prayers of the faithful to God, went so far as to destroy the relic of healing and the emblem of salvation. The lesson which he taught has constantly to be re-learned. We are still in the wilderness, and we tend to false emphasis; even to false worship.

The religious who is faithful to prayer—real prayer and not merely to the fulfilment of the obligation or to the correct kneeling position when being seen by others—will find little difficulty in distinguishing between the words of monasticism as a means and the work of monasticism as an end. Humility discovers the difference between the superficial and the real.

Where the soul has greater need of light is in deciding how much of the external is to be retained and how much rejected. There is a danger that a soul, newly enlightened as to the delusion which fidelity to the external practices of religion may well become, will discard too much of the external as being inferior, elementary, and evidently misleading.

Here again it is only love that provides the test. Both means and end must be seen in terms of love; their value must be measured by nothing else. Love is the two-edged sword which separates the essential from the accidental, and the accidental from the superstitious or exhibitionist.

It is only in the gradual development of the life of prayer that the soul comes to learn this love, comes to see with this light, comes to make these decisions. Just as the soul that is in the wrong way of prayer becomes increasingly unsettled, increasingly at the mercy of impulse, increasingly unsure, so the soul that is in the right way of prayer begins more and more to have the feel of truth and reality.

It is by the indirect effect of prayer rather than by the direct effect of reasoning that the soul's values undergo these significant changes. The light of grace discloses to the soul with humiliating clarity that the satisfaction which had hitherto been experienced in the religious life has been largely a matter of taste and emotion.

The carefully constructed monastic ideal, coloured and captioned and suitably lit, is seen in the life of prayer to have been a projection of self. It is not that love has been left out, but rather that love has been misinterpreted. It is not that sacrifice has been left out, but that it has been identified with hardship.

It is only in the light of prayer that the soul comes to know the meaning of divine love. And love, in its turn, teaches the soul the secret of true prayer. In the knowledge supplied jointly by love and prayer the soul grows in wisdom, stability, and supernatural obedience. It is now that the monk begins fully to see the purpose of his vocation and the spiritual value of his rule.

Together with the grace of a religious vocation goes the grace of a truly supernatural approach to the works of the religious life. But such is his freedom and his folly that a man may respond to the one while refusing the other. A man may remain a monk, may follow the routine of monastic life, may never dream of reproaching himself, may even be held up as a model to others, and may yet be completely missing the implications of his vocation. This would be impossible if he sincerely prayed.

The reason why prayer is so important here is that, apart from its primary purpose, which is to give glory to God, it deepens the life of faith and love. Faith and love develop proportionately, being fed by grace received in prayer.

Much faith is required, and much love too, of course, if the vocation to religion is to be followed up with generosity. Faith not only lays the foundations at the beginning of the spiritual course but is the only refuge when all else appears to fail the soul in the more advanced stages. Even faith appears to fail at some points, but it remains the one refuge nevertheless.

The security which rests on faith and is formed in prayer is the peace which is promised by Christ and which is unobtainable from the world. But then you would expect a security coming from divine wisdom to be different from that which comes from worldly wisdom.

Love, prayer, and faith so interact as to be almost indistinguishable in their articulation. In the sense that prayer speaks for love and faith, it is their articulation. But whether formulated or not, prayer is the worship given by faith and love. It is this that the service of religion is designed to promote.

So much, then, for the aim of religious life: the glory of God, personal sanctification in union with Christ and according to a certain pattern as defined by rule and vows, the cultivation of the theological virtues, and the development of the life of prayer.

On the serious desire to strive after the ideal just outlined the whole life of the religious rests. We have seen that the desire must be realist and not romantic, God-centered and not self-centered, informed by grace and not by the senses. We now have to see in what practical ways the religious life rises to meet this ideal.

If the foundations of the monastic life, partly idealistic and partly practical, are neglected, the building will be either abandoned before it is finished or else so overcrowded with activities as to be indistinguishable from the secular buildings which surround it.

What we have to do is to find the principles common to most religious orders and examine them in the light of love, prayer, and faith. To agree on the foundations is at least a start.

In the dual purpose of 'searching after God' and 'departing from one's own will' which can be taken as fundamental, the first condition or disposition is custody of the heart. For the ordered love of God, which is what the vocation purposes, there must be an ordered love of creatures. Not *no* love of creatures—which would make it virtually impossible to work for souls or to study or to pursue a creative art—but no inordinate attachment to creatures, which is a very different thing.

In this there is again a negative and a positive element. The negative demands the renunciation of disordered affection, the positive offers a heart-free oblation of praise. To be emptied of the wrong kind of desires is supernaturally ineffectual unless the soul can be filled with the right kind. The monk must have something to put in the place of passion or his service will be bloodless and sterile.

Custody of the heart touches other fields besides those that relate to people. True, the danger of particular friendship is the first to be guarded against in religion—especially when many confessors seem to think that because two people are bent upon loving God there can be no great harm in being fond of one another—but if it is proposed to love God with the whole heart, *any* other claim upon the affection must constitute a danger.

Precisely because the members of a community are pledged to divine love, the movements of human love are to be held all the more suspect. A speck in the eye, says Suso, is just as harmful to a man's sight if it is a speck of pure wheat or a speck of black cinder.

Nor is the excuse valid that allows the religious to attach himself to those whom he wants to convert or improve. Surely the more a man wishes to do good to people supernaturally the more he should deny himself the pleasure he finds in them naturally.

'If you stop at something', says St John of the Cross, 'you cease to give yourself to the All.' In the same way if you stop at one person you cease to give yourself to the many. '*Humanum cor tanto intensius in aliquid unum fertur*', says St Thomas, '*quanto magis a multis revocatur.*'[3]

A monk who is at the mercy of his feelings and attractions is not

---

3   The human heart is more intensely borne towards one object in proportion as it is withdrawn from many others.

tending towards the perfection which is expected of him in the terms of his vocation. He is not expected to be without feelings and attractions—the insensitive do not make the best religious—but he is expected to rise above them. The monk has a heart, and he may not turn it into a stone; but he must not do all that it tells him.

Man's sensitive nature responds instinctively to the stimuli of created and transitory good. God could have willed a humanity which was impervious, but in fact has willed one which is susceptible. Creation being as it is, man has to learn from Him in prayer how to handle his natural reactions to created good.

'Nobody is able of his own strength', says St John of the Cross, 'to empty his heart of all desires.' And it is the desires, not the objects of desire, that are the real obstacles to freedom of heart.

In the last analysis all man's problems and most of his sufferings spring from his desire for joys and possessions that fall short of the capacity of his heart. The fleeting and the second best do not satisfy him, so he is forever aching over his own emptiness.

The soul that inordinately desires creatures, whether it is a question of people or comforts or possessions, will never be able to find rest in God or stability in prayer. 'The reason why some have no inclination towards virtue,' says St John of the Cross, 'is that they entertain attachments which are not innocent nor directed towards God.'

'Let us have great care even in the smallest things,' says St Teresa, 'once we feel an attachment, to withdraw our thoughts from the object that captivates us, and to bring them back to God.' Detachment is absolutely necessary if there is to be order in the soul, and order is absolutely necessary if there is to be love.

'*Ordinavit in me caritatem*', sings the bride in the Canticle showing us that love which is not ordered is no love.[4] Detachment is the condition of the soul's attaching itself to God alone. Ordered love can come only as the gift of grace. It is in prayer that the soul learns the love that orders love.

Charity is the only thing in the world strong enough to stifle the desires that oppose it. This is because charity comes from God and

---

4   He hath ordered me in love.

goes back to God, while the other desires come from fallen nature and from the world. And God has overcome the world.

The heart of the monk, if it deviates from the love of God alone, can become an unquiet evil. It wanders, looking for rest and finding none. It fastens on other hearts and drains them of the love of God. If it shrivelled up in solitude it would be a waste enough, but the heart that has tired of the love of God and that hungers still for love is a menace.

Freedom of heart means detachment from holy things as well as from holy persons. In religion the soul has constantly to be repudiating the good in order to mount to the better. It is not possessions that constitute the greatest snare—because it is easy to detect this kind of acquisitiveness—but rather the goods of the intellect, and even the goods of the religious life itself.

Thus, the heart must be kept free from the satisfactions to be derived from work, ambitions, success, and even penance and prayer. These points will be dealt with on a later page; enough to note here that the good attaching to study, works of zeal, external activity of any kind, is not so great as the evil attaching to self-will. Where there is more of greed than of good in any work undertaken in the name of religion, nothing is added to the glory of God. Unless it can be purified, it had better be dropped.

If even religious activities can take away from the purity of a man's heart, it stands to reason that secular activities can do so even more readily. A monk must see to it that he is detached from his non-community recreations—from entertainment, sport, worldly reading, listening, and seeing. Nor is it always honest for him to say, 'I take these things with thanksgiving. I enjoy them. They are worldly, but not sinful. I am detached from them. After all it is the spirit in which they are approached that matters.' This may express a defence mechanism; it may be sheer humbug.

A monk does not have to renounce every pleasure, but he has to make sure that he is indifferent to every pleasure. Custody of the heart and of the senses means that he is ungreedy in every pleasure, that he refers his pleasures to the test of God's will, that he examines his pleasures in the light of higher needs and the calls of grace.

The Pauline criterion of accepting with thanksgiving covers only one appetite—and that which has somehow to be satisfied anyway—but there are other instincts in man besides that which is met by food. If gratitude to God is taken to be the sole test it can become a screen and a formula. There is no guarantee in St Paul's concession that so long as we say 'thank You' to God we may freely choose our literature, freely witness films, freely listen to broadcasts.

Another basic principle which is assumed in all religious rules is the surrender of personal preferences to the wish of superiors and the custom of the house. It is not here a question of submitting to the *will* of the superior, or to the *rules* of the house—this would come under the head of obedience in the strict sense—but is rather a question of letting one's life be moulded by the Spirit of God as revealed in the spirit of that environment in which He has set it.

Not only does the religious life rest on this submission of the will, but it is to a large extent conducted from day to day on the strength of it. The indifference which it engenders is one of the conditions of pure prayer, and it is also the disposition most necessary for community life. It relieves the soul of many distractions and anxieties, it rises above controversial questions on monastic policy, it cuts out planning and ambition.

If we need to have our charity set in order, we need also to have our submissions set in order. The surrender of the will must be ordered towards God and not towards the line of least resistance, towards the more lax interpretation, towards evasions and escapes.

The resulting calm is not the calm of inertia, the sterile aloofness of the fatalist. It is the tranquillity which comes of order. The soul is receptive but never passive. Faith cannot be passive. To search after what is known, and in the direction that it is known to lie, is one of the few activities that make for peace.

There is humility in the exercise because the soul has to take it for granted that superiors and the community—let alone Divine Providence—must know better than the individual subject what is required of this particular form of religious life.

There is fraternal charity in the exercise because the soul is constantly having to defer to others and to make allowances. If religious submission means anything at all, it means that the monk has to follow the will of others and not try to push it along with his own.

In searching for the will of God which is to spell for him his sanctification, the monk must know in faith that the life to which God has called him is the frame of his perfection. It is in this and in no other that he finds his terms of reference. '*Gloria et divitiae in domo ejus.*'[5] Though the treasures in the house are for the most part hidden, the monk will not find them by pulling down the walls.

A third principle basic to the conception of the religious life would be single-mindedness. In its monastic context this quality includes simplicity, stability, integrity, and unworldliness. It includes a number of other qualities as well, but these will be discussed when we come to treat of the vows and of community life.

The religious who does not develop in his life this attitude of inward and outward unity will find himself constantly drawn to change his approach to the essentials of his vocation; each new wave of enthusiasm will bear him off, only to land him on a new rock. For the religious vocation to produce supernatural results there has to be an established outlook which no mere mood may alter.

Multiplicity can spoil a religious vocation. It affects the life of prayer, overloading it in the beginning and inducing disgust for it in the end. It affects work for souls, undertaking more and more commitments which must inevitably lead to extroversion, complication, distraction and dissipation.

Without fixity of purpose there can be no real serenity. For prayer the soul must be free of the hundred preoccupations which excite the mind of the unsimple man. The man who is not simple in this sense is all the time having to reconcile one duty with another, one loyalty with another, one ideal with another.

Unless the soul is set towards a clear objective there is the danger that in occasions of decision the judgment will wobble. The purely spiritual may find itself passed over in favour of the expedient; in the

---

5   Glory and riches are in his house.

absence of a single purpose, self finds a multiple of good excuses.

The fourth fundamental principle of monasticism to be considered here is conformity. Arising out of the other three, it means roughly the willingness to behave as a member of the community, to fall in with the ideas of authority, to be regular in observance.

The aim in this is to eliminate singularity. Any sort of freelance endeavour, however apostolic and praiseworthy, cuts at the roots of both obedience and the common life. For the monk there is no safety apart from the corporate. He prays, works, eats, recreates, does penance as part of the life of the house.

The things done by monks, no less than the things used by them, are the property of the community: their acts are not private. Not that these acts need necessarily take place in common, which is anyway not a question for the subject to decide, but that no act of the monk is an independent act: nothing apart from, still less opposed to, the general directed effort.

Weariness of monastic routine can induce a monk to find escape in regularized isolation: permission can be extracted from superiors to do almost anything that does not involve sin or scandal.

Fidelity to the practices of the house, which includes the horarium but goes beyond it, effects a solidarity among the brethren which is necessary if fraternal charity is to mean more than smiling at one another in the corridor. Without this regularity in observance, which sees to it that for the significant elements of their vocation the members of the religious family meet together at stated times, charity can become selective and therefore to a large extent natural.

Also, in providing an atmosphere favourable to prayer, a day-to-day norm is essential. Stability was not invented simply to prevent monks from wandering from monastery to monastery; it looks to the question of recollection as well, ordering the events of the day so that prayer has a chance of becoming a settled habit.

Such then in brief are the foundations of the monastic life. Treated in text-book form as above, they appear formidable, uninviting, multiplex. But so do the foundations of anything—a house for instance—appear when you look down into them from the level.

You do not have to spend much time examining the foundations of the house once you have chosen to live in it. You do not have to remind yourself, every time you move from room to room, that they are supporting you. But you do have to know that they are there, under you day and night, and that only in proportion as they are truly laid will they take the weight of whatever is put upon them.

Activity undertaken on insufficient training can be too much for the structure. 'How shall they preach unless they be sent?' How shall monks mix with men unless they have withdrawn from men? How shall monks teach unless they have been taught in prayer?

If the scheme outlined in this chapter is felt to be complicated, we can only insist upon what was suggested at the beginning: namely that the Rule, like the Gospel, proclaims a Person. We live not so much according to a code, to a list of regulations, but rather according to the example of a living Prototype and according to grace.

If Christ is not the alpha and the omega of the life, if Christ is not the 'yesterday and today and the same forever',[6] there is no particular point in monasticism. Indeed, a fairly good case could be made against it.

The argument is very simple: the soul learns Christ by living like Christ, and this it is the aim of religious life to teach. The soul loves Christ by loving like Christ, and this, too, it is the aim of the religious life to teach.

At first it might seem that God has many attributes which He wants served and imitated, has many causes which He wants furthered, has many claims which He wants recognized. But when we come to know more of His ways with men we see that the thing is not so complex. From Him to us, and from ourselves to Him, it is ultimately an exchange of love.

'I have loved thee with an everlasting love,' says the Lord in Jeremias, 'therefore have I drawn thee.'[7] This is the whole story of the religious vocation. From now on it is a matter of letting oneself be more and more drawn in love.

---

6 Hebrews 13:8
7 Jeremias 31:3

3

UNWORLDLINESS

IN his chapter on the instruments of good works, which are the means he gives for the attainment of perfection, St Benedict requires of the monk that he keeps himself from the ways of the world ('*a saeculi actibus se facere alienum*'). Nor is this a piece of casual pious advice thrown in for good measure among a lot of others. The saint returns to the idea several times later on.

Throughout the Rule there are warnings against worldliness. St Benedict's insistence on enclosure is precisely to safeguard the spirit of unworldliness and recollection. Not only must the monks' excursions into the world be strictly limited, because in the saint's words '*vagandi foras omnino non expedit animabus eorum*,'[1] but those who have been outside for one reason or another are forbidden to tell their brethren when they get back what they have seen or heard while they were away.

That St Benedict considers contact with worldly people harmful to the souls of his monks is further seen in the provision which he makes for the doorkeeper of the monastery: only a man of mature formation is to be appointed to this office. A monk with one foot still in the world would easily, if he had to see much of secular guests and callers, be swept off the other.

Even more telling evidence of St Benedict's mind is shown in the

---

1 Wandering afar is in no way expedient for their souls.

terms of the vow *conversio morum*[2] which is taken by those of the Benedictine following. *Conversio morum* (or *conversatio morum*) demands a clean break from the secular life hitherto lived. By it the monk pledges himself to strive after perfection according to a new pattern and as a convert from the habits of the world.

The vow in question means more than the willingness to pick up the novitiate tricks. It means more than shedding the characteristics and fashions of contemporary life. It means being ready to learn new modes of expression, to assimilate new and supernatural values, to train oneself in what has been described as monasticity of manners.

Conversio morum is in effect a vow to banish, in desire and so far as possible in memory and in practice, the whole range of worldliness from the soul's horizon. Eyes that are focused to the screen, to the restaurant, to news-print, can hardly be expected to read the more subtle signs of God's intention.

Since it is always God's will that the monk is looking for His will, the need to keep the perceptions of the soul sensitive to the spirit is paramount. Because spiritual perception is dulled by pressures of the world, the world, with all its natural excellences as well as with all its false sanctions and ephemeral attractions, must give place to the spirit. *Conversio morum* aims at securing the unworldliness which rises above the pull which goes on pulling when the devil and the flesh are in abeyance.

The trouble about renouncing the world is that it comes back in another form. You bar the window of your cell against it, and it comes up through the boards of the floor. You throw it out by the door, and it comes in through the ventilator.

Cutting off from the world is not like getting rid of possessions. The renunciation of money and goods can be tested by merely checking a list. Cutting off from the world is turning your back on a whole sweep of ideas, emotions, desires, daydreams and hopes. It means cutting yourself off from much that is yourself.

By deciding seriously to renounce the world you are renouncing what is inside yourself as much as what is in the world outside you.

---

2   Conversion of manners.

Outside the monastery lies the material world with its machinery for advertising material pleasure. Inside the monastery, within the enclosure of your own mind, lies an even more partisan world which issues unremitting propaganda about self.

The unworldly monk, the monk who lives according to grace, is no longer being shaped by an environment which is hostile to the spirit. He has to a certain extent escaped the tyranny of creatures. Not altogether escaped it, because he will always be subject to the life of sense so long as he is in the body, but at least he will be living on top of creatures instead of underneath them.

The worldly monk, on the other hand, the monk who has clung to the nature which may have been all very well as regards the obligation that was owed to God before he came into religion, is torn and distracted. He is bringing the past into the present, and this never answers.

By bringing the world with him into the cloister, by trying to grow up into a new man while determining to retain his old self, the monk condemns himself to frustration and misery. He is not a natural religious or a supernatural one. Nor is he a man of the world. He is two people, neither of whom is quite normal. He is a Siamese twin. The circulation of grace does not flow properly. The digestion of the particular kind of spiritual nourishment which monasticism is supposed to provide is hampered. In the end there will probably be a breakdown.

Leaving aside the Holy Rule we find the same idea in the psalms. If we would enter into the service of God, the psalmist tells us, we must forget our kindred and our father's house. And in St Paul: 'Your life is hidden away now with Christ in God. Christ is your life ... you must deaden, then, those passions which belong to earth .... you must be quit of the old self and the habits that went with it, you must be clothed in the new self, that is being refitted all the time for closer knowledge, so that the God who created it is its pattern.'[3]

In practice how shall I ever rid myself of my worldly side, of my pre-vocation habit? I find that I betray myself constantly in my way of talking, writing, laughing, standing and walking. Though I renounce

---

3   Colossians 3:1-5

worldly topics of conversation, I catch myself out in my eagerness to hear other people discuss them. Though I renounce newspapers, I am glad enough to see headlines.

When, in the terms of the Epistle to the Corinthians, shall I discover myself to be a new creature in Christ, my old life having disappeared and everything about me new? The answer is that I probably never shall. But though I may never know how far I have triumphed over the world, the fact that my spiritual life is deepening me *in Christ* will give me a share in *His* triumph over the world.

I should find as I go on in the spiritual life that the cumulative effect of prayer, abstraction, lack of worldly entertainment and news will at least reduce in me the mundane. But so long as I willingly meet worldly people and draw my circle of friends from among them, so long as I feed my mind with worldly interests, I cannot expect to fulfil my vocation as one who is called to leave the world.

Unless the withdrawal is physical and actual there is no guarantee that it is anything else. What is the use of saying, 'In the will I have left the world, and it is the spiritual that matters'? If a monk allows himself worldly conversations, worldly literature, worldly music and games, how can he deepen his life in Christ and preserve recollection, let alone defend himself against the philosophy of the world?

Neither prayer nor an attitude of mind comes of its own accord. The grace of prayer has to be supported and safeguarded; so has the unworldly way of looking at life. For the undiscriminating there can be no fixed attitude of mind; and very little prayer.

'Thou didst leave me for eleven days,' says St Gertrude to our Lord, 'and it appeared to me that this happened on account of a worldly conversation.' The experience of this Benedictine saint is significant, not only because it reveals the effect which this particular impact had upon her mystical life, but also because it shows to what a degree of discernment her habitual unworldliness had brought her that she should recognize so clearly these causes and signs in her soul.

Unless the spiritual man sets his face against every form of mundane influence his vision will not be acute enough to read the signals by which God means him to be directed. We have seen that where there is no discrimination there is no fixed attitude; it is equally true that where there is no fixed attitude there is no discrimination.

But what, it might here be objected, if my work as a monk places me among people of the world and outside my enclosure? Surely I cannot lose the finer touch in matters of the spirit when I am only doing what I am told? By acting under obedience, am I not proof against these evils of which you speak?

Obedience is not magic. The virtue of it covers a good deal, but not everything. Granted that obedience compensates for any loss suffered by the soul in its association with the world, it does not pretend to block out impressions which are left by association with the world.

It is like the elixir of Frère Gaucher: distilling his invention under obedience did not prevent the inventor from becoming a drunkard.

Submission is, as we have seen, fundamental. The whole structure of the life, whether viewed spiritually or constitutionally, turns on the attitude of the monk towards authority and authority towards the monk. This means that the sacrifice of worldly pleasure is not so pleasing to God as the sacrifice made in the name of obedience. Nobody would deny this. It is nevertheless an inescapable fact that the images taken away by the mind as a result of moving in a worldly element are of themselves harmful to the soul. No word of command can alter that. The word of command can justify it—can even sanctify it—but it cannot alter it.

Then the burden of responsibility rests wholly with the superior? No, not wholly. Authority has of course to take the major share—that is what it is for—but the subject has his obligations still. When authority has spoken, the subject must go ahead. But in doing so he must know that his obedience has not bandaged his eyes, stopped up his ears, anaesthetized his heart. He must know that his imagination and memory, those trickiest of faculties, will be more lively after his incursion into the world than before.

Though superiors may take it upon themselves to expose a subject to worldly influences, the subject still has to hold himself to account for the custody of his senses. It may go very much against his own choice that he has to mix with the world, but it is his own senses that are mixing and nobody else's, and he has charge of them.

So if on my return from a journey which was not of my choosing I find myself distracted and unsettled, if through having to deal all day with seculars I find myself fumbling with the problems of the interior life, if after teaching boys over a period of time I find myself adopting the idiom of the world and forgetting my 'monasticity of manner', I am in part to blame. In part only, but still to blame. The degree of blame is exactly measured to the amount of self I managed to extract from the obedience which sent me mixing with the world.

It might be argued that apart from the merit of obedience there would be the merit of charity in leaving the enclosure for the sake of people outside it. Ought we not to sacrifice our monastic ideas to the much more important idea of the Gospel? In the light of love for one's neighbour, does not love for one's enclosure appear somewhat sectarian?

The answer to this is contained in what you mean when you talk about vocation. To some it is given to be apostles, to others not. To some it is given to live in the world, to others it is given to live in monasteries. 'Live according to what you are' is the scholastic axiom, 'and you will grow.' If you are called to be a monk, you have to have very good reason to be found walking in the world.

There will of course be occasions when the demands of charity necessitate interludes spent in secular surroundings. But it would be as wrong for a monk to seek out such occasions as it would to make worldly use of such occasions when they are legitimately presented.

'A man with the monastic spirit,' writes Abbot Delatte, 'should never solicit the favour of returning to his home.... Those men most greedily desire converse with people in the world for whom such people are most dangerous.' In another place, and as emphatically: 'The tables of layfolk were not made for us; neither their wines nor their talk suit us.'

It is sheer delusion to imagine that we can do good to souls by going against the character of our vocation.

To lessen the differences which separate us from men of the world may bring momentary successes. But the good cannot last. Those whom we imagine we are helping in this way either cease to respond after a while or become frankly disillusioned in their ideas of the religious life. And we harm our own spirit.

Religious who belong to monastic orders, and more especially those who belong to contemplative orders, do more for souls by keeping withdrawn from the world than by going out of their way to convert the world.

'If the time I might spend in paying visits,' says St John of the Cross, 'is spent by me in my cell begging our Lord to inspire the people to do what they ought, then why should I pay visits apart from those required by charity or necessity?' The same saint, in a passage that has become famous, claims that one act of pure love does more for the glory of God, for the Church, and for souls than countless acts of zeal. Monastic orders exist for the purpose of eliciting acts of love.

Accordingly, it is easy to see why St Benedict stresses the need to keep all things necessary within the enclosure, why he wants those of his monks who have to leave the monastery for a time to take the spirit of the cloister with them, why he dislikes his monks accepting meals when on their journeys (so expects them to come back if possible during the day), why he forbids correspondence without permission, or the giving of presents. The whole tenor of the Rule is towards separation.

Even where he is regulating for behaviour within the monastery, St Benedict shows his desire to widen the gulf between the ways of the cloister and the ways outside. He makes a great point of custody of the eyes, he utterly banishes buffoonery and lightheaded laughter, he insists that there should be nothing elaborate about either the clothing or the food, he does not let the brethren call one another by their Christian names alone, he expects a certain gravity in their movements about the house.

In all this it is not repression for the sake of repression. Modest deportment as such is not holy; if anything, it is rather depressing and irritating. The reason why it is given so important a place in St Benedict's scheme is simply that it proclaims to all—to the members of the community themselves as much as to guests and people outside—the religious nature of the life and the necessity of taking rigid practical steps to secure the environment of prayer.

According to the original conception, monks are people who are separate, set aside for God, and the more they recognize this themselves, and by their behaviour bring other people to recognize it, the better for the state of religion.

Always the monk must remember that for him the world is as alien an element as the sea is to man. He is out of his depth in the world. Potentially—not inescapably but potentially—he is a drowning man. Though obedience may throw him in, he does not become a fish. In order to keep afloat he has to make greater efforts than those who are in their natural element.

But at least he can comfort himself with the knowledge that for the sea to get the better of him, it has to be swallowed. It is not strictly the extent to which a man is in the water that causes drowning; it is the extent to which the water is in him.

The same principle may be applied to activity of any kind in the life of the religious, not merely to worldly activity. It is not necessarily the amount that a man takes on that matters; it is the amount of it that gets inside him.

We religious, afraid of being left behind in contemporary thought, assent too readily to the conclusions of a humanist and materialist society. We yield to persuasions without bothering to ask for credentials. It all happens too smoothly. The movement of the world slides over our preference for spiritual things, and we wake up to find that we have accepted earthly things at the world's valuation.

It is only the wisdom of the spirit that can show up the more hidden errors contained in the world's propaganda, and to possess our share of this wisdom we have to pray. Prayer alone insures both the light to see and the strength to resist.

The religious who lets his prayer go accommodates himself, while still directed towards the eternal, to the temporal. In order to live by faith a man will need all the grace that ordinarily must come to him through prayer. If he does not live by faith, he lives by sense—which is worldliness.

To those who live in eternity while still on earth it signifies little if they are out of date, ignorant of current fashion. To those who are building the city of God, the gossip of the streets is of no account. To those whose lives are modelled on the life of Christ, the mannerisms of the world are passed over, are of no concern. Such souls have the ways of Christ to imitate.

4

POVERTY

THE appropriate expression of unworldliness is voluntary poverty. It is idle to pretend that you have broken with the world if you sit surrounded by its luxuries.

Voluntary poverty does not guarantee detachment, but it is intended to denote it, help towards it, crown it. Poverty is to detachment what silence and solitude are to prayer.

Granted that the desire to possess does more harm to the soul than the possession itself, religious poverty is directed against both the desire and the object of desire.

St John of the Cross says that the soul suffers 'greater unfitness if it has the smallest desire for the things of this world than if it were burdened with hideous temptations'. And in another place: 'The soul that is attached to anything whatever will not attain to the certainty of divine union.'

It is for the letter of poverty to keep a check on what is owned and used—on the 'anything whatever' of the above quotation—and it is for the spirit of poverty to purify the will. It is easier to examine ourselves on fidelity to the letter than on fidelity to the spirit. Fidelity to the spirit is more difficult to acquire.

It is an error to imagine that if we look after the one, either the letter or the spirit, the other is looking after itself. It is easy to believe that we have the spirit of poverty when in fact we are nowhere near it. The test, as in all virtues, lies in what we are prepared to do about it.

In the same way we can think that by keeping the letter we are being faithful to poverty when in fact our wills are still burdened with attachments.

While the spirit of poverty cultivates the unpossessive attitude of mind, the letter sees the attitude of mind translated into act.

It is not so much that the spirit is theoretical and the letter is practical; it is rather that the spirit of poverty informs the fact of poverty, and that the two work together to make up the complete virtue.

Thus, so long as material things are possessed, the presumption is that the owner wants to possess them. Such a one is not practising poverty either in spirit or in letter. If he wants to acquire poverty as a virtue, he must begin by facing poverty as a fact.

So, in spirit and in letter, poverty finds its necessary place in the conception of the religious life. There can be no religious life without renunciation, and what St Benedict calls the *'vitium proprietatis'*[1] is one of the first things to be renounced.

Though monks of the Benedictine tradition do not explicitly vow themselves to poverty, they are pledged by their state as religious to its observance. What St Benedict thought about the obligations and virtue of poverty is evident from a number of places in the Rule, and we know from St Gregory's account of his life what importance he attached to its practice. So, like chastity which again is not vowed by Benedictines, it is contained by implication. The vows of obedience and conversion of manners, if nothing else, demand it.

So, where St Thomas says that 'religious by vow bind themselves to abstain from temporal, even lawful, things so that they may attend to God more freely,' he is stating the principle of poverty not only for non-monastic orders but for followers of St Benedict as well.

To free the religious from servitude to material things is the object of holy poverty, and unless a man is looking for this freedom he had better stay in the world and not take the vow.

For a man to hanker after the stage effects of poverty, and not after

---

[1] Vice of ownership.

the greater liberty to attend to God, which is the purpose of religious poverty, is only to place himself under further servitude to material things. He is now a slave to the patched habit and the bare cell.

Free to attend to God, the religious has confidence in Divine Providence for his material support. The virtue of poverty is then twofold in its virtuous effect: it directs the soul to worship and elicits the act of trust.

'Take no thought for your life what you shall eat, nor for the body what you shall put on ... seek the kingdom of God, and all these things shall be added to you.' Poverty does not stop at getting rid of things.

The blessedness of poverty lies not in its nakedness and indigence, but in its complete surrender and confidence in God. Once the religious has really no thought for the morrow, the actual doing without will give him little trouble.

He will accept the necessaries of life without question as coming from the hand of God. He will even expect them. He will give thanks for them. But he will not want to be weighed down spiritually by the unnecessaries of life. These he will reject.

It may be that even the necessaries of life, or what he considers to be the necessaries of life, are denied to the religious man. It is not often that destitution is the lot of a religious, but when it is the man who possesses the spirit of holy poverty will see it as more of a privilege than a privation. 'The Son of man has no place where he can lay His head.'

To submit without complaint or self-pity to the decree of God's Providence which takes away more than one was prepared to give is far more purifying than the sacrifice of those things that in fact one gave.

The process of denuding is carried out in two stages: there is the early part where the soul strips itself, and there is the later part where God does the stripping for it. Both stages are meant to hurt, but the second part hurts more.

In all voluntary renunciation there is inevitably an element of self. It is I who am choosing to renounce myself, and it is I who am choosing what to renounce. Where the renunciation is a necessary one, occasioned by circumstances or by the will of a superior, it is all of God and there is no room for self.

Such renunciations have a twofold merit: as being chosen by God they bring more grace to the soul than if chosen by self; as being accepted and suffered in virtue of a poverty voluntarily undertaken, they bring graces of their own, graces attaching specifically to the state of religious poverty.

The value of poverty to the soul is measured, then, by several qualifications. It will depend upon the detachment from desire which the soul brings to the work of actually shedding material things, upon the confidence which is placed in God for the supplying of what is necessary, and upon the day-to-day suffering of the consequences. It is the day-to-day suffering of the consequences that provides the surest standard of measurement.

If it is how we show up when we are in need that we learn the quality of our renunciation, then the more we are in need the better. We have here a yardstick which we cannot afford to neglect. But let it be a genuine need and not an inflated one.

The advantage which the poor outside in the world have over most religious is that they are genuinely in want. Among religious the need, though at times pressing, is to a certain extent fabricated. This is inevitable. If the monastery or religious order is rich, the individual religious is bound to feel secure. The need will have to be of his own making.

Security of some sort is essential to conventual life. If the community labours under constant financial anxiety, the end for which it exists is almost impossible of realization. And where there is security there is the tendency to depend, if not on riches, at least on less than God.

Though the element of want may be absent as regards the monastery, there is no reason why it should be absent from the life of the monk. Though it may have to be fabricated, it does not have to be fictitious.

Religious poverty, whatever the endowments of the house, can be real enough to those religious who do not mind going without the things which, even as religious, they are entitled to expect.

In the practical sphere this would mean, not only cutting down non-essentials, such as smoking and obtaining money from superiors for entertainment and subscriptions to newspapers and periodicals, but also seeing whether the essentials are as essential as they seem.

Is it essential to my life or only to my comfort that my cell is equipped as it is, that my wardrobe is stocked as it is, that I have this number of books in my care and that number of stamps to account for? Is it essential or merely convenient that when travelling I take just as many meals as people in the world, that I take wheeled transport when I could manage on foot, that I choose the more expensive way when the poor of the world have to travel cheap?

Monks should not enjoy a higher standard of living than that of people in the world. Religious poverty is meaningless if they do. The fact of being dedicated to the service of God does not entitle a man to live at greater ease than his neighbour. Rather the reverse: he is expected to show evidence of self-denial.

The religious who thinks he should be better housed, better fed, better dressed than the working man has no spirit of poverty. The fact that more often than not he will be better off in these ways than the working man should be to him a matter of humiliation. A religious should feel ashamed when his state, which requires the vow of poverty, relieves him of its practice.

In order to counter the evil of private ownership in the monastery, St Benedict does two things: he decrees that 'all things be common to all', and at the same time puts the common goods of the house on a strictly supernatural level. The combined effect of this must discourage the brethren from 'treating the possessions of the monastery in a slovenly or negligent way'.

The saint's argument is that the monastery is 'the house of God', and that all things in it have to be handled with respect. Everything that is put at our disposal is in a sense sacred; we are to regard the *vasa monasterii* as being *altaris vasa sacrata*.[2]

In the light of this the monk has to ask himself whether the ob-

---

2   Vessels of the monastery as being the sacred vessels of the altar.

jects for which he has obtained permission and which he uses daily are not in fact used as though they were his own private possessions, are not thought of as being on a quite different level from the candlesticks, the altar cloths, the missal.

How would I feel if something which has been given to me for my use—it might be a typewriter, a chisel, an alarm-clock—were assumed to belong equally to anyone else in the house? Yet according to the Holy Rule the object is for common use, is only borrowed by me from the treasury of *vasa sacrata*.

Nothing could be more emphatic than St Benedict's *'neque aliquid habere proprium nullam omnino rem'*.[3] The monk who judges it to be an invasion if his pen is taken without his consent should consider the words of his holy founder, *'neque codicem, neque tabulas, neque graphium, sed nihil omnino'* can be called his own.[4]

But in all this we must remember that true religious poverty lies in being, not only materially poor, but poor in spirit. The ideal is to detach ourselves from all that is our own, from the selfhood which possesses and absorbs and calls for more.

The ideal is to free us from self-importance, self-interest, self-pity. It is the *proprium* in us that poverty is designed to attack, the self-will that fastens on anything it can get and that blinds the soul to what is being lost.

'God abandons to the nothingness of their pretended riches,' says Abbot Marmion, 'those who, believing that they possess something, trust in themselves; but His infinite mercy fills the needy, who hope only in Him, with gifts of grace.' 'Let us try to act in such a way,' says the same Benedictine on the subject of poverty, 'that through prayer and through our eyes being ever fixed on our Model, all our motives may be supernatural.'

Thus, the solution of our problem of holy poverty lies, as you would expect it to lie, in Christ. He who said *'Venite post Me'* was answered later on by St Peter in the name of all religious with *'Reliquimus omnia et secuti sumus Te'*.[5]

---

3   Nor to keep anything whatsoever as their own.
4   Neither book, nor writing tablet, nor pen, nor anything whatsoever.
5   'Come after me' and 'We have left all things and followed Thee.'

Souls whose whole desire is to identify themselves with Christ cannot but be sharers of Christ's poverty, lovers of Christ's poverty. A living faith in Christ is the surest safeguard to the ideals and observances of poverty. It is the mistake of religious that they try to work from poverty to Christ when they would do better to work through Christ to poverty.

If God were truly our whole happiness we would count it part of that happiness not to be tied by material things. '*Quid mihi est in caelo, et a te quid volui super terram?*'[6] But because for most of us God is only part of our happiness, the other part is spoiled by the demand that creatures make.

The peace of soul which is offered by our Lord and St Benedict alike is bought only at the price of sacrificing creatures. 'Every creature appears as insignificant', says St Gregory, 'to the soul that contemplates the Creator.'

In contemplation the soul learns the due order of God's creation: material goods are the servants and not the masters of men, men in their turn are servants of God and not rebels against Him; the senses are subject to the will, and the will is subject to God.

'*Et ita omnia membra erunt in pace.*'[7] Commenting on this sentence from the Holy Rule, Abbot Marmion says something which epitomizes the Benedictine concept of religious poverty, indeed of the religious life: 'Peace is the fruit of detachment; the soul has no longer any disquietude; it belongs altogether to God.'

---

6 'What do I have in heaven, or what do I desire upon earth besides Thee?' — Ps. 72:25
7 And so all the members shall be at peace.

5

CHASTITY

FROM voluntary poverty the mind that looks for means of serving God goes on logically to the idea of voluntary chastity. It is next in the scale of renunciation: having surrendered his goods, the neophyte surrenders his body.

Because bodily pleasure plays an important natural part in man's well-being, its absence leaves a legitimate craving unfulfilled. If man were animal only, this craving could not, since animals have bodies without souls, be met other than by physical satisfactions.

But since man is partly animal and partly spiritual, a way of living has to be developed which subordinates the lower appetites to the control of the higher. The grace of God makes such a development possible.

If the grace of God did not make this possible, and even make it perfect, no religious would dare to take the vow of chastity. If it were possible without the grace of God, no religious would need to.

Religious chastity, then, is at once a free offering to God and a free gift from God. Theologians are agreed that without the grace of God it would be impossible for a man to retain his innocence: the virtue of chastity is a grace.

Before the fall, chastity was instinctive; it came naturally. Since the fall it has to be preserved, and preserved with difficulty; it comes supernaturally. St Thomas says that man needs supernatural help to do what our first parents did by nature.

The fall has brought such opposition to chastity that we need great grace even to see it in its proper light, let alone to resist the opposition. As with every other virtue, it is only those who cultivate it who can see it for the virtue that it is.

In a fallen world we tend to think of chastity as the negation of certain sins. It would be more correct to think of the sins as the negation and privation of chastity.

The spouse in the Canticle is spoken of as 'coming up from the desert, flowing with delights, leaning upon her Beloved'. Untouched by the smoke of the cities, she is wholly pure: her disposition matches that of the Beloved Himself, and she leans upon His virtue.

It is no good trying to explain this to the libertine. He may understand chastity as a refusal to give in, as something unbroken; but he will not see it as a grace. He will not see the strength that chastity gives to the chaste. He will not see it as *virtus*—power as well as virtue.

To the unchaste no exposition of perpetual continence is convincing; to the perpetually continent the exposition is assumed.

Where the Exemplar is rejected, the example of chastity is either not credited or else witnessed unmoved. It may even be ridiculed. See Christ and you cannot but see His purity: see His purity and at once you see the significance of other people's, and its genuineness.

But grace does not operate by itself. The spiritual side of man's nature has to be so developed as to maintain its mastery over the physical side. Grace builds on nature; it does not act as a substitute.

Neither poverty nor chastity is a label that is attached to the religious on the day of his profession, entitling him to the other half of the beatitude. The initial impulse has to be fed by further grace, the habit has to be established and deepened.

Man's lower nature, never wholly tamed since it emerged from the jungle which it made of Eden, is always waiting to spring. The eyes close, but the flesh never sleeps. You think you have chloroformed the flesh with its vices and concupiscences when perhaps you have provided merely an interlude of refreshment.

Reason, fear, foresight, watchfulness—all these things help. But prayer and penance help far more. Prayer and penance relate directly to love, and chastity is love's special province.

The soul that loves God will take chastity in its stride, will assume it, will not entertain the thought of anything else. But love does not come automatically. It has to be prayed into us.

When the soul is directed toward God, when the intellect and will are intent on the same object, when the emotions are ready to forgo their disturbing tendencies, the body has little chance of rebelling. While prayer is the vital force in a man's life, and love is his whole aim, the senses may have nuisance-power, but they will not be strong enough to reverse his purpose.

The body gets its grosser satisfactions only when higher up in the scale of man's faculties there is disunity or laziness or contradiction. The building of the tower of Babel went ahead while all spoke the same tongue.

It is when the interior appetites do not tell the same story that the exterior appetites take advantage of the discussion and assert a similar right to independence.

The record of civilization bears out the truth that whenever the body is cultivated beyond a certain point, the spiritual and cultural level of society declines. If man's physical attributes could accept without arrogance honours which properly belong to the spirit, there would be no problem. But enshrine the flesh, and the spirit is deposed.

Safety can lie only in encouraging the interior life to such an extent that outward things begin to lose their hold. 'If the soul, taking lawful delight in spiritual union with God,' says St Thomas, 'abstains at the same time from seeking pleasure in union with creatures outside the bounds of divine order, then that soul is spiritually chaste.'

In the terms of the above quotation there is an area within the divine order where creatures may be enjoyed, and an area outside it where they may not. For the religious, the area of lawful enjoyment is considerably smaller than the layman's.

That this restricted terrain of physical well-being be kept holy, the particular graces of the sacraments are required. It is not altogether a matter of mortifying the passions, a subject which will be treated in the next chapter, but is even more a matter of strengthening the soul in the sacramental life.

Though each of the sacraments promotes chastity among the other virtues, the two sources of strength on which chastity most relies are baptism and Holy Communion. (The sacrament of matrimony may relate more immediately to one aspect of chastity, but it does not come within the scope of the present purpose. Confirmation, penance, and orders supplement as regards chastity the work done by baptism.)

By baptism a soul is consecrated to God, acknowledging His Fatherhood and finding incorporation into the life and body of His Son. Baptism is an initiation which alienates a man from his former self, transferring whatever right he had to the ownership of God.

'Know you not that your bodies are members of Christ', St Paul explains to the Corinthians, 'and that you are not your own?'[1] Body and soul, we have left our own dominion. 'You are the body of Christ', repeats St Paul in a later chapter.[2]

If God had done no more than create us, He would have right of possession over us as His creatures. But being members of His Son we belong in a new way. And if as Christians we are not our own but His, as religious we belong even less to ourselves. We have no rights at all; His possession of us is complete. 'You are bought with a great price'—the price of Christ's Passion which merits for us our adoption into the family of God and which provides for us the grace of our religious vocation—'glorify therefore God in your body.'[3]

It is in this way that our baptismal dedication, working through and implemented by our religious dedication, feeds the chastity that we profess. Failure in a religious to live up to the implications of chastity is an assertion of rights which do not exist. It is a misuse of property which belongs to someone else—to God.

But God is not merely the divine proprietor of His creatures, He is the divine Father. Man is not divinely appropriated merely, he is divinely loved. 'I have loved you with an everlasting love, therefore have

---

1 1 Corinthians 6:15, 19
2 1 Corinthians 12:17
3 1 Corinthians 6:20

I called you that you should be Mine.'[4]

From our human experience we know how even the association of love can invest an object with an interest which of itself the thing does not possess. God does not associate love with us: He loves us. So if we are loved by God we acquire a value out of all proportion to what we otherwise would be. There is something related to us in God upon which we can absolutely depend: His love cannot refuse us. He endows us with it.

Again, from our human experience we know how much of ourselves we put into the things that we love. We impart something real about ourselves, we project into the objects of our love something which does not belong to anyone else. We are what we love, and the things that we love are in a sense ourselves.

If our love for God is at all like our love for people, and if His love for us in any way follows the same principle, we, as objects of divine love, must bear a singular responsibility and grace.

Clothed thus in divine love, how can the mind do otherwise than love chastity? 'My spouse is a garden enclosed, a fountain sealed', sings the shepherd in the Canticle.[5] Chastity reserves the soul, mind, imagination, and body for God. 'Thou art beautiful, O my love, sweet and fair ... how full of loveliness thy steps.'[6] Chastity moves everywhere with grace.

Raised by a divine love to a dignity not known where the lower passions are consented to, even the purely physical side of man is made worthy. Where the senses are purified, taking their chastity from the chastity of the mind, 'this body begins to put on here below', says St Cyprian, 'something of the spiritual and glorious state promised to the risen faithful.'

Born of divine love, the chaste soul and senses must be held to their birthright by the sacrament of divine love which nourishes them in grace. The food of Christian life is Christ Himself, given to man in the Holy Eucharist.

In proportion as the eucharistic life is developed in the soul, chas-

---

4   Jeremias 31:3
5   Canticle of Canticles 4:12
6   Canticle of Canticles 4:1

tity is both safeguarded and enriched. It is not that Holy Communion is meant to act as a miraculous relic or medal, banishing the evil of impurity in return for reverent reception; it is rather that with every reverent reception of Holy Communion the human character is built up till it more and more resembles His.

The closer a man comes to the likeness of Christ in love the further he separates himself from the evils, within and without, that threaten his chastity. The saint, the man who is so identified with Christ as to leave nothing over which is of self, has come to have chastity in his nature.

Such a settled habit and practice of chastity have little to do with human nature which is fallen; it has everything to do with the nature which is risen in Christ.

With the grace of the Holy Eucharist, then, crowning the graces of initiation and dedication, it should not be too difficult for the religious to serve God in perfect chastity.

In both holy poverty and holy chastity, the religious reflects Christ hanging upon the cross. Each has love as its inspiration, end, and meaning. 'Blessed are the poor in spirit … blessed are the clean of heart.' In embracing poverty, the religious makes Christ his whole support; in embracing chastity he makes Christ his whole love.

Though poverty and obedience are the frequent theme of sermons, the ideals of chastity are seldom preached. Yet of all our religious obligations, that of chastity is perhaps the hardest to fulfil perfectly.

The Fathers spoke and wrote about chastity—witness St Augustine, St Athanasius, St Ambrose, St Cyprian, St John Chrysostom, and also Cassian and the fathers of the desert—but in our own time we hear mostly about impurity.

It is true that St Benedict in his Rule makes only four references to chastity, two of which are indirect, but this is because his plan is not so much to preach or instruct as to legislate. Chastity needs less legislation, the broad terms being once laid down, than almost any virtue.

No abbot can dispense his monks from chastity or any part of it: it is binding on all of them and all the time. The perfection of its observance, it is true, as also the guilt of its infringement, can admit of degree. But the ruling principle of chastity could hardly be more clear: it demands that we love what our lower natures hate, and that we hate what our lower natures love.

This being so, St Benedict does not make chastity the matter of vow; he prefers to reserve his three monastic vows for material less essentially bound up with the moral law. Certainly, the allusion which he makes to the necessity of rejecting immediately the least thought against the virtue clears him of underestimating either the ideal of chastity in the monastic life or the reality of the temptations against it.

In the case of the three vows which are taken by Benedictines—namely obedience, stability, conversion of manners—insignificance of matter would render the transgression venial. So also in the question of poverty. But where it regards chastity, the matter is always grave, and any transgression is mortal. This negative evidence shows us, if nothing else does, at once the sacredness and sensitiveness of chastity.

In order to resist sins which are excused from being mortal only by deficiency in deliberation, knowledge, consent, a soul must have great confidence in God. Complete trust is the only way. Given this in a soul, all else follows: ideals, safeguards, actual graces to meet actual temptations. This lacking, and the soul is left to natural strength of character—which is not enough.

'Chastity is impossible', says Cassian, 'unless the foundations of humility are laid in the heart.' Knowledge of our weakness can be the source of our strength. It is only the man who sees how powerless he is to meet the evil that surrounds him who throws his whole care upon God. Power, God's power, is made perfect in acknowledged human infirmity.

The lifelong practice of perfect chastity calls for heroic virtue. But so does the lifelong practice of anything else that is to the glory of God. The religious, moreover, in undertaking to serve God in the terms of his vocation, bargains for heroism.

Monks and nuns have been described as 'witnesses to the Absolute', and shall witnesses fall short, in intention anyway, of the absolute chastity which is there for them to see and reflect?

6
EXTERIOR PENANCE

AFTER chastity the next thing to consider is the quality which, short of the direct action of grace, most helps to preserve it. The readiness to mortify, or chastise, the flesh is the first step; to mortify, or chastise, the will is the second. The words *castitas* and *castigare* have an affinity: they derive from the same stem, they suggest similar ideas, they supplement one another in end and means.

To prevent ourselves from pampering the body we have to chastise the body. If we do not chastise it, it will, with its constant demand to be pampered, chastise us. Even when we weaken, listening to our lower nature, we get no peace: our higher nature reproaches us.

Mortification does not exist for the sake of chastity alone. It is needed as a corrective in the function of every sensitive appetite. It comes into every department of the religious and interior life. Particularly it affects poverty, humility, obedience and charity. It is difficult to see how any of the vows can be kept without it.

It is strange that in the religious life, where all are striving after the same thing, there should be divergent views on such a central element of the vocation as voluntary mortification. Some in religion would even deny that voluntary mortification holds a central place at all, holding that it is an accretion, that it externalizes a principle which relates to the interior, that it can be passed over without spiritual loss.

Against this stand the Gospel, the Holy Rule, and centuries of practice in the Church.

In the first Christian centuries the faithful were encouraged to chastise the flesh to an extent which would now be counted for morbid exaggeration. The world approves of every extravagance except religious extravagance.

But the love of God is essentially extravagant. The service of God exaggerates: it outdoes the service of anything else. Saints are fools for Christ's sake. The preaching of Christ crucified, St Paul tells the Corinthians, is 'to the Jews a stumbling-block and to Gentiles foolishness'.[1]

The folly, the extravagance, of the cross is the highest wisdom. It is the way chosen by Him who is the Way. It is the way of truth and life as planned by Truth itself and Life itself. The folly of the cross is a revelation of Wisdom.

What the world calls stupidity, at least religious should recognize as congruity. To act in harmony with the life of Christ it would appear only reasonable that a man should take up practices of self-denial.

In order to get the most out of whatever hardship he suffers it would appear only reasonable that he should study the principles of Christian asceticism. For a religious, on the grounds that his ordinary duties provide him with all the mortification that he needs, to dismiss the whole question of voluntary self-denial as irrelevant is to admit that he sees only half the point of it. The part that he sees may be the more important part, but the other deserves practical and prayerful consideration.

What such a man does not see are the finer shades of generosity. He misses the distinction between voluntarily accepting the hardships of his state and voluntarily embracing them.

The monk who argues that nothing more can be required of him than the fulfilment of his obligation as a religious would be the last to argue that because his community supplies him with all the conversation he needs, he need never speak to anyone outside it, that because he is supplied with all the food he needs he has never any occasion to eat anything else.

The links between what is voluntary, what is necessary, and what is

---

[1] 1 Corinthians 1:23

lovingly undertaken must be clearly seen. If the connection is missed, penance is viewed either as a tyranny or as a matter of personal taste.

It is not as though God, whip in hand, were standing over His human creatures as a slave-driver. He does not compel us to fasten the manacles about our wrists. He invites. 'I, if I be lifted up, will draw all men to myself': draw, not force.[2] Freely we offer Him our penance, and He takes it. We can go on offering more and more. We can offer Him our intellects and our wills. But even when we have given Him our whole will, and He has taken it, we are still free.

We can bind ourselves irrevocably, but we are still free. If God took away our freedom, He would be depriving us of our service as well as depriving Himself of our service. A service that is inevitable, necessary, physically determined, is without love. A love that is compulsory is no love. There would be exaction but no sacrifice.

Penance where there is no spontaneity, where the subject is not free, might conceivably be useful in keeping at bay the occasions of sin, but if it is to help in spiritual progress the act must be assumed by the soul with at least some degree of deliberation and with the intention of atoning for sin.

'If any man has a mind to come My way', we have it in the most recent and authoritative translation, 'let him renounce himself, take up his cross, and follow Me.'[3] Those who choose to be My disciples, our Lord is saying, must choose to do penance.

The rich young man chose not to be a disciple. He was free to refuse. We are not told that by refusing to come Christ's way, by not renouncing himself and following, he lost his soul. All he seems to have lost was his happiness and his proffered perfection.

Christ, confirming the statements of the Baptist and the prophets, tells man that his sins need expiation. He takes the burden of reparation upon Himself. But it does not end there: He asks that there be others to weep together with Him; He does not wish to tread the winepress alone.

There is a debt of honour which man owes to God. God leaves man to fulfil it or not, as he chooses. Some take upon themselves the

---

2 John 12:32
3 Luke 9:23

burden of penance and find it light; others leave the whole weight to Christ. 'I chastise my body and bring it into subjection', says St Paul: *he* does the chastising, God merely gives him the grace to do it.

St Benedict gives the doctrine of Christian asceticism in a sentence when he says that the monk is 'to deny himself in order to follow Christ'. If the Father has ordained that we go to Him only by walking in the footsteps of His Son, then cross-bearing and the avoiding of all that might get in the way of reaching Him must form a major part of the journey.

The mind of St Benedict on the question of renunciation and corporal penance is perfectly clear. The monk is not to admit soft living: '*delicias non amplecti*'. On the contrary, he is to punish the body: '*corpus castigare*'. His is to be the traditional form of penance, namely fasting: '*jejunium amare*'.⁴

The whole life of the monk is to have about it a certain Lenten character, and during the actual season of Lent there should be further stress upon the penitential aspect of the monastic vocation. The monk should ask permission of the abbot to make additional restrictions in matters of food, sleep, and conversation. If this is the view of St Benedict, it is only reflecting the view and practice of an earlier monasticism. 'Ought not Christ to have suffered, and so to enter into His glory?' Ought not monks to suffer, and so to enter into their—that is, His— glory? Monks belong to Christ, and 'they that are Christ's have crucified their flesh with its vices and concupiscences.'

So the monastic doctrine in relation to penance turns, according to St Benedict, on the monk's identification with Christ: '*Passionibus Christi per patientiam participemur*.'⁵ Patience here means more than enduring without irritation.

Having seen what Christ, St Paul, and the Holy Rule outline for us in the way of motive and ideal, we must now come down to the concrete practice. What are the particular observances suggested, and how are they to be performed without falling into one or other of the mistakes to which ascetics are liable?

---

4 'Not to embrace delicate living'; 'to chastise the body'; and 'to love fasting'.
5 That we might through patience share in the sufferings of Christ.

If our Lord laid special stress on the need for fasting in the expulsion of evil spirits, if He Himself spent forty days of fasting in the desert, if He said that when He, the Bridegroom, should have left them, the disciples would have to fast and do penance, there can be little doubt as to which of the corporal penances most claimed His blessing.

The connection between prayer and fasting in the Gospel, between fasting and watching throughout the Scriptures, puts the renunciation of food on a level higher than other forms of corporal renunciation.

It seems that fasting and vigil, more particularly than the use for instance of the discipline and the hairshirt, go before man's greatest religious adventures. The combination is seen in the case of Moses preparing to receive the Law, of Elias before receiving his vision on Horeb. Judith, Daniel, Tobias, Esdras and David fasted and watched in preparation for significant events in their lives.

This idea of waiting and doing without nourishment is reflected in nature: the field lying fallow and waiting for the season's rains, the seed relying on its inward reserves during the underground vigil before growth, the snake fasting before sloughing its skin, certain animals fasting before the mating season. Where there is to be a new mode of being, there is deprivation. Resurrection has to be preceded by renunciation. You could probably find symbols in nature to typify walking barefoot and sleeping on boards, but they would not be as telling as those that speak for fasting and watching.

Certainly fasting is given first place among penances by the Fathers. Though most of them have something to say about its necessity and power, St Basil and St Jerome are its particular advocates. Two of St Basil's homilies are devoted to the practice of fasting, saying how it strengthens strong men, begets prophets, gives wisdom to lawgivers, safeguards the soul.

St Jerome goes further: 'If you wish to be perfect, it is good not to drink wine or eat flesh ... the drinking of wine and eating of flesh and fulness of stomach make a seed-plot of lust ... reason must be present that we may take food of such a kind and in such a quantity as will not hinder the free movement of the soul.' In another place the same saint lays down a doctrine which may be extreme but which is in the authentic tradition: 'Our bodies need only something to eat and drink. When there is bread and water and the like, nature is satisfied. Whatever more there is, does not go to meet the wants of life but only ministers to vicious pleasure.' It is true that St Jerome is here addressing those who are aiming at high perfection.

But are not all religious aiming at high perfection? Even for souls who are not by their state set aside for God and pledged to renunciation, there is penance to be done. 'What was lost by excess'—to quote St Jerome for the last time—'was regained by abstinence: a proof that by fasting we can return to Paradise whence, through fulness, we have been expelled.' (While the immediate reference is to the re-writing of the tables of the Law, the application was intended to be general.)

With so much to go surety for the honour of fasting, it is not always easy to preserve a sense of proportion. A well-intentioned soul might make the mistake of specializing. Without the direction of obedience, fasting can become something of a mania.

The idea of fasting for the love of God was not invented by spiritual writers as a substitute for dieting. Once it becomes an excuse for dieting, it is dieting, and there is nothing supernatural about it.

To insure against any one ascetical practice becoming a hobby, a man must see how he is placed in relation to the rest. More important still, he must see how he is placed as regards the whole question of interior mortification, which will be discussed in the ensuing chapter, and as regards obedience.

Ascetical writers are agreed upon an order to be observed in the practice of mortification. It is given here not because it is particularly enlightening—the sequence could hardly be otherwise—but because it provides a practical working guide. Also, the findings are good for one's humility.

The relative value of penances is coldly estimated by the experts as follows: first come the mortifications which the Church prescribes; next, those that are demanded by the Rule or that arise out of the daily life in the monastery; lastly, such as are self-imposed. In all this it is to be understood that the trials sent by God are of greater value to the soul than any that are undertaken by choice.

Among trials that are sent by God may be numbered both unavoidable ills—such as physical pain and illness, loss of friends, interior desolations—and impositions which come in virtue of obedience and charity. Thus, on two counts, as coming from God and also as coming from the nature of the monastic obligation, a move to a less congenial work, or a snub received from one of the brethren, is to be preferred to a voluntary fast or a voluntarily assumed hairshirt.

The reason for the pre-eminence of the Church's discipline over any other is not only that her authority carries greatest weight. The reason is a more theological one. In fulfilling the Church's penitential requirements, the faithful help 'to fill up those things that are wanting to the sufferings of Christ'—sufferings which are complete in Him as Second Person of the Blessed Trinity but still incomplete in His mystical body which is the Church.

The penances which we perform because the Church tells us to are assimilated not only into the wealth of the mystical body's existing but unfulfilled passion, but also into Christ's infinite, measureless, perfectly adequate and meritorious Passion.

Though we may derive less sensible satisfaction from keeping the Church's discipline than we do when we fashion and keep our own, at least we know for certain that our share of the debt is being honoured in Christ's name: our propitiation, in virtue of His, is good.

The reason, again, why our observances of the Rule are more pleasing to God than those of our own devising is that by our profession we have renounced independence, and that whatever we endure in community has the character of a dedicated act.

In religion we may not look for escapes from the crosses that come to us as we might have been able to had we stayed in the world. We may not, or should not without necessity, resort to palliatives. We have voluntarily taken on the life, together with whatever trials that might come, and now the trials are not voluntary but necessary.

The trials supplied by the ordinary routine life within the enclosure do more than anything else to advance the soul in humility, patience, charity, regularity. If they are evaded, independence comes back, and with it countless failures in obedience, stability, and conversion of manners.

For the Benedictine, one of the most serious immortifications is love of change. In secular life a spirit of restlessness can lose a man his career; in monastic life it can lose a monk his vocation.

Benedictines—and this goes for Cistercians, Carthusians, and those who follow St Benedict's Rule—have to resist the least stirrings of *Wanderlust*. By their vow of stability which obliges them to remain, unless sent out by their abbot on some special work, in the monastery of their profession, monks renounce the right, and as far as possible the desire, to remove to another house. Except in the case of volunteering to make a foundation, the Benedictine does not think of altering his surroundings or his work

The monk who is weak in stability, who does not seriously try to mortify his love of change, will reveal a weakness in a number of other monastic virtues as well. Self-chosen excursions into the world are against the spirit of poverty as much as against that of stability. Freelance works of zeal, extra-claustral in character and in fact, are against the spirit of community life as well as against that of stability.

One of the chief antitoxins against monastic immortification, whether the particular serum is worldliness, singularity, extravagance, or love of variety, is the rule of enclosure. It would be difficult to say which is helped more, prayer or penance, by the keeping of enclosure.

Always admitted that compunction of heart is more of the essence of penance than outward austerity, physical correction and deprivation of some sort must nevertheless come into the soul's scheme of religious service. An asceticism which is purely spiritual, which looks down on the other as elementary and inferior, is to be held suspect.

There can be self-deception in every department of the spiritual life, but the self-deception which suggests that the soul has risen above the need for corporal mortification is one of the most dangerous. The next stage is to claim that the soul has risen above interior mortification as well.

The two run parallel. Show me your discipline of the mind and you show me if your discipline of the body is according to God or not. Show me how you go about the work of mortifying your flesh and you show me the quality of your interior asceticism.

So long as Christ's Passion is its inspiration, each aspect of penance is valid and sanctifying. 'Thus it is written that penance and remission of sins should be preached in His name among all nations.'[6]

---

[6] Luke 12:47

7

INTERIOR PENANCE

THERE is the denial of the senses and there is the denial of self. A man may deny his senses for the sake of his health, his appearance, his finances, or for a number of other reasons; it does not follow that he is denying himself. Such a man is denying one part of himself so as to satisfy another part. To deny oneself is, in the present context, to deny one's whole self so as to satisfy God.

Thus, the purpose of Christian self-denial is to submit to God the inward and outward faculties, and thereby re-establish in Christ the order disturbed by sin: surrender, suffering, reconciliation. It was because our first parents were not fully surrendered to God that their wills rebelled. Estrangement and disorder can give place to union and order only when the price of suffering has been paid.

It is not the Christian ascetic alone who preaches this truth; the pagan philosopher sees the same necessity. 'When we break away from order through some fault,' says Plato, 'we can return to order only through suffering.'

Not until the soul is at peace within itself can there be perfection of virtue or perfection of happiness. With the gift of the beatific vision the peace at last becomes absolute; but even on earth the soul may receive the gift of peace. It is the peace of Christ, and it comes through the Passion of Christ—the Passion in which the soul must be ready to take its share.

Cultures other than the Christian have known that order, whether in the mind or in society, is the sole foundation of peace. The Greeks sought to order man's environment with a view to his *eirene* or state of tranquillity; the Romans saw peace as order imposed by authority, either by law or arms; the Jews understood peace to be a gift from God, an order in the soul and in the race, arising out of a covenant between Yahweh and His people.

So it is only when history follows the Hebrew concept of peace and order—the Jewish *shalom*—that it comes near to appreciating the truth. The peace which the Messias was to bring, the peace which the prophets have foretold, is God's gift of grace, of love.

Peace as understood in the Old Testament is something which is forfeited by the disorder of sin. Where God's covenant is violated, there is chaos. With the New Testament, or Covenant, comes Christ who is our peace. In Himself, and for love of man, He reconciles humanity to His Father and restores order where before was the disorder of sin.

'Through the blood of Christ you have been brought close,' writes St Paul to the Ephesians, 'you who were once so far off. He is our bond of peace. He has made the two nations one in Himself.' The pax Romana which was secured by submission to authority is turned into an interior harmony resulting from an interior submission. The philosophical and aesthetical peace of Athens becomes a theological fact. Even the peace of Jerusalem and the prophets is raised to a new level. 'Christ has put an end to the law with its decrees, so as to make peace.'

Writing still to the Ephesians, St Paul goes on about 'Christ's message being of peace for those who are far off or near, who are united in the same Spirit.' Union in the same spirit is another term for order.

But though this peace which Christ brings is, as the prophets foretold, a grace from God, it is nevertheless a grace which comes only when the soul has disposed itself by establishing inward order. When the due subordinations have been made, the soul may confidently dwell in the peace of God. But not until.

For the sake of order in the soul, which means ultimately for the sake of divine love, a man should be ready to make any sacrifice. The man who is not ready to make any sacrifice that God may want of him will never find full love or peace. The man who is ready will have to show it by sacrificing certain exterior and interior satisfactions.

We have seen above how mortification of the senses is not an exercise of supererogation but of necessity; we come now to see that the same is the case in regard to mortification of the will. Exterior discipline is a sign, an earnest of what the soul is hoping to do next for God, a goodwill gesture, a preparation, a novitiate. The real renunciations are those to come, the renunciations of the spirit.

'Beware of limiting the good of fasting to mere abstinence from meat,' says St Basil, whom we saw to be a champion of outward austerity, 'real fasting is alienation from evil.' St Athanasius, also an apostle of asceticism, says much the same: 'See how much a fast can do, and in what manner the law commands us to fast. It is required that we do so not only with the body but with the soul.'

If the senses of the soul correspond to the senses of the body, and are of far greater importance than the senses of the body, it follows that they have to be similarly purified and far more carefully. Which means far more painfully.

One thing which adds to the difficulty of mortifying the interior faculties is that they are invisible. It is easy enough to keep a check on whether or not the sense of touch or of sight is properly under control; it is not so easy to tell whether we are sufficiently controlling the appetites of intellect and will.

Another factor which renders the assessment of interior mortification more difficult is that the greater the penance, the less it is seen as penance. (In the case of the exterior senses it is more often the reverse: the sharper the discipline, the more clearly it is recognized.) For example, to see frustration and loneliness as penances, which in effect they are, is harder than to see as penances the suppression of a malicious criticism and the readiness not to make excuses.

It is an almost invariable rule that the trials which are of most value to the soul are those which seem to be doing least good. We have not chosen them, they do not fit our frame of spirituality, we would rather suffer anything else in the world, they must be sheer waste of time and even occasions of bitterness and resentment. They are to the glory of God all the same.

And why? Because God has chosen them and we have not, because they fit into His frame of spirituality and not into ours, because He would rather we suffered these particular trials than any other in the world, and that the sense of waste, bitterness and resentment is the mere spitting and spluttering of the sacrificial fire.

The feeling that he must, by his want of patience, be spoiling the work of God in his soul is one of the special trials which the tried servant of God will have to suffer. The conviction of failure in cross-bearing is allowed by God, is indeed insisted upon by God, for the necessary purpose of hiding from the soul the value of the suffering. It is the preservative of humility.

True penance and spiritual self-sufficiency do not mix, so in order to secure a spirit of true penance in the soul God takes away from it all consciousness of its merit. And since there has to be some evidence in the process of self-condemnation, or the soul might suspect that it was being treated like a child, the emotional and purely superficial rebellions, inflated out of all proportion by the imagination, are allowed to persist.

The penances most pleasing to God, then, are not always those that man chooses to make to Him. It is not for man to say what things he wants to sacrifice to God. If he does this, it can only mean that there are things which he wants not to sacrifice.

Nor is it given to man to see into his own will and to know the degree of willingness with which he sacrifices. It must be left to God to measure the purity of a soul's penance: all that the soul has to do is to make sure of the motive and the direction. It is best that the quality and the reward of penance be hidden from the soul.

Nor, again, is it given to man to see into the mind of God and to know the degree of satisfaction that his penances have given Him. It is a great penance not to know that one's penances have been so much as acknowledged. What God wants of some souls is the sacrifice of knowing that there has been a sacrifice.

Repeatedly it must be insisted that the essence of true interior penance is the disposition on the part of the soul to yield blindly to whatever sacrifices God may require of it, and to the manner in which God may require them. This is the soul's entire concern, and any sacrifices that are made in such a disposition cannot but be pleasing to God. Put in another way, the disposition *is* the sacrifice: it is the living immolation of self, which is penance.

It was the continuous, unretracted, perfect oblation of self that made the life of Christ an uninterrupted act of love. It was not only with the Passion that Christ started doing penance for man's sins.

'For Thy sake,' says St Paul to our Lord when writing to the Romans, 'we are put to death all day long.' This cry from the penitent heart gives us the principle of Christian asceticism and mysticism combined. The love of God is a consuming fire: it goes on consuming, and what is offered is still there to be burned.

'I die daily', and every morning I wake up alive for further death. If death to sin and to my own corrupt desires were a clean death, final and sealed, it would be so much easier. I would see my new life rising like the Phoenix from the ashes. But instead, I have to go on being put to death all day long.

It is not surprising that this text from the epistle to the Romans is taken up by St Benedict and made the basis of his teaching on the subject of penance. Seven out of the twelve degrees of humility relate explicitly to penance: indeed, they are as much appeals to penance as to humility.

'Reckoned as sheep for the slaughter', quotes St Benedict in his fourth degree of humility, continuing the same verse from St Paul. This marks the first stage in the progress of penance: the soul receiving with resignation the trials that God sends. Led to execution by the force of circumstance, we are 'put to death' willingly. Not eager to meet our punishment, but at least not rebelling against it. Physically shrinking, even emotionally shrinking, but with the will accepting. With the will refusing escapes.

The next stage comes when 'for Thy sake' we accept the cross with gratitude. Recognizing the privilege of bearing the cross with Christ and for Christ, the soul begins to welcome chances of proving itself worthy. In the earlier stage, as a sheep, the soul was passive; now there is active cooperation.

When the soul moves on in generosity and can invite the consummation of the sacrifice which was in the terms of the initial dedication, then is the third part of St Paul's claim verified. 'All day long' the soul is intent on serving God in penance. At no time does the soul want to be satisfied with creatures. 'My whole occupation', it sings with the Canticle, 'is love.'

In this third, and highest, degree of penance the soul is the living witness to Christ suffering. The arms are outstretched to receive the cross, and if persecution and contempt in fact follow—though essentially it is the attitude towards suffering that God wants—they confirm the likeness and bring added glory to God.

All acts of penance, however small and whether interior or exterior, performed in this third disposition are of great merit. The reason for this is that whereas before, in the earlier stages, there was room for motives of vainglory and self-esteem, now, when the soul wants only what is according to Christ, every act of penance is an act of love.

So love comes to be the touchstone of penance: it discovers pride and fear at once, and rejects them. Love overcomes fear, and the humility which is born of love overcomes pride. On this whole subject, whether you think of it as primarily to do with love or humility or penance or order, nothing could be put more clearly than the principle stated in the concluding paragraph of St Benedict's chapter on humility.

'When these degrees of humility have been mastered, the monk will come to that love of God which casts out fear; to that love whereby everything which once he observed by fear he shall now begin to do naturally ... for the love of Christ, out of good habit, and from delight in virtue. All this our Lord will work by the Holy Spirit in His servant now cleansed from defects and sins.'

So the perfection of penance for the monk is to be found in his deliberately choosing to live a life of suffering in preference to any other for the sole reason that Christ has immortalized this particular form of life as being the fullest expression of love.

Thus, the higher the soul aims in the mounting of love, the greater will be the suffering. But proportionately greater will be the grace to make the suffering bearable. The fact that with the progress of love, order is more and more established in the soul, and together with order the extending of an interior though very often secret peace, must have the effect of building up a natural as well as a supernatural courage. Certainly, the soul has nothing to fear. The consequences of aiming high in love will be something to be thankful for, not something to dread.

The impulse to love in the first place has come from God, and shall God now deny the graces that make the crowning of that love worthwhile?

The order, the peace, the courage, the light, the opportunity—all these things are graces, so many tokens of God's love—and shall God deny the culmination to which everything in the soul aspires?

'*Ordinavit in me caritatem*': it is to be able to say this and know that it is true—to be able to see it with the objective wisdom of the bride in the Canticles—that is the hope of the soul that is learning to love. 'He brought me into the cellar of wine, he set in order charity within me... his left hand is under my head, and his right hand shall embrace me.'[1]

Leaving the question of approach for that of actual performance, we are up against a difficulty not so manifestly present in the case of exterior mortification; namely, the difficulty of temperament.

In the correction of gluttony or stopping too long in bed, the question of temperament scarcely enters in. A piece of straightforward self-abnegation meets the problem. But where there is a need to mortify a bent for melancholy, for criticism, for restlessness and romantic wanderings of the imagination, you are faced with a more subtle problem. You have to correct not only a habit but a nature, a temperament.

Since we have made our habits, we can unmake our habits. We have not made our natures, so we cannot unmake them. Both belong to us, habit and temperament, so we shall have to give an account of them; but whereas our temperaments are formed for us, our habits are formed by us. Interior penance is necessary in either case.

---

1   Canticle of Canticles 2:4, 6

Sometimes interior mortification gets as far as correcting the bad habit but stops short of correcting the bad nature which produces the bad habit.

For instance, it can virtually stamp out the tendency to gossip or to lose one's temper while leaving the mind still free in temperamental tendency to curiosity and anger. The outlets are only half the story, and though we are obviously more responsible for the outlets which we allow than for the natures which we possess, our most serious effort should be directed towards the right ordering of our temperaments.

I cannot be blamed for inheriting the temperament I possess; I can be blamed for not controlling it. My personality may be either a gift or a curse. I have had no say in its origin, but I have every say in its management.

In the crisscross of motives and desires and dreads which is myself, I must unravel as much as I can see and put order where there is confusion. I must purify and supernaturalize. I must dispose it towards Christ. I must learn to 'put on Christ' and to 'walk in Christ'. All this will need light, all this will need burning away much that is rotten.

But where there is generosity, where the heart is right with God, the light is assured and the work of burning away is brought about in spite of temperamental flaws and imperfectly corrected habits.

A soul that wants to love God, and that tries to show that it wants to love God by resisting cynicism, rash judgment, discontent, vanity and ambition, will not be deprived of love by default of penance. If penance should still be wanting, God will exact it secretly in the form of suffering.

It is now that the soul must be more careful than ever in its interior self-denial. To indulge in self-pity at this stage will spoil the work of God in the soul. Silence and complete surrender in the hands of God must be the policy. 'You should complain to no man', says the Carthusian writer Lanspergius, 'of those crosses that you suffer.'

Complain not only to no other, but not even to yourself. Complain—if complain you must, though it is more perfect to keep silent—to God alone. Accusation endured without exculpation calls for the highest virtue: the restraint of Christ before Pilate sets the ideal of Christian endurance.

What we are apt to forget is that Christ renounced, not only the right of self-defence, but also the refuge of self-pity.

It requires the most searching of interior penances to purify the soul of self-pity. Even though it may never be outwardly expressed, the desire to stay hurt and lonely in a suffering is a weakness which cries out for attention and correction. To cling to a misery is to cling to self.

To the soul that truly loves Christ there is only one misery, and that is sin. Neither disappointment, misunderstanding, persecution, waste, the ingratitude of unfeeling men, nor any of the other horrors to which temporal life is liable need constitute a misery. There are no grounds for it; sin is the sole grounds.

If it is our sin, or other people's sin, that is the cause of our wretchedness, there is always an immediate remedy to be found in Christ. Christ is our refuge; self-pity is never our refuge.

To nurse our spiritual bruises, particularly when the suffering or the sin is no longer there, is to nurse ourselves. Men who would not dream of wallowing in feeling ill and giving the supposed illness as an excuse for avoiding unpleasant duties, will often wallow in their sense of misery and excuse themselves from being pleasant.

The danger of spiritual hypochondria is greater, among spiritual persons, than that of its physical counterpart. Its presence is not so readily recognized, and as a rule there is nobody else in a position to see it and warn against it.

At the same time, it is not to be expected that in every suffering, particularly if the suffering has been unmerited, all sense of hurt and self-commiseration can be eliminated. There are occasions when the memory goes on smarting from a sense of injury, when the imagination builds up armies of attack. But it is not the emotions that are the test; the test is to be found in the intellect and the will.

Where the intellect agrees, if only in the darkness of faith, to the rightness of the suffering, and where the will, again perhaps acting blindly but on the strength of the intellect's assent, decides to accept the suffering to the glory of God, the soul is well disposed. Memory and imagination will, when they have let off steam, come under control.

For reasons given above it is better that the soul should not at once appreciate the harmony of parts that the combined effect of industry and grace is bringing about interiorly. Just as in the case of voluntary self-oblation the soul is prevented from seeing itself sweetly sacrificing, so here in the case of voluntary suffering it is prevented from seeing how the faculties are being marshalled into position.

Feeling within itself the sighing of self-pity, the humbled soul cries out: 'Joy I have mastered, but I cannot master sorrow ... and sorrow is a passion like any other.'

The answer is in St Paul, where he says to the Colossians: 'Your life is hidden away now with Christ in God. Christ is your life ... you too will be made manifest with Him in glory.'[2] In Him is everything fitly jointed together, every member helping member, every part contributing to the perfection of the whole.

With us, until our natures are properly organized and our habits well under control, it is different. A spasm of joy, fear, anger, lust, sadness, and at once we are thrown out of the true, out of harmony.

In nearly all our sufferings it is not the occasion itself, the actual thing endured, that hurts us and upsets our balance; it is the effect of a certain circumstance upon a sensitivity not quite ordered.

Accept that circumstance and you are with Christ; you are bringing order into your soul; you are making for peace.

Accept *all* circumstance, any contingency that God may choose to arrange, and you echo Christ's prayer in the Garden: in faith and hope and love you are taking on the Father's will in whatever form it may express itself.

'Mortify therefore your members which are upon the earth':[3] this, assuming its purpose of reparation, is the first duty of penance, and is carried out under self-inflicted acts of deprivation. 'Walk in the Spirit and you shall not fulfil the lusts of the flesh. If you are led by the Spirit you are not under the law ... and they that are Christ's have crucified their flesh with its vices and concupiscences ... if we live

---

2   Colossians 3:3-4
3   Colossians 3:5

in the Spirit let us also walk in the Spirit':[4] this is the second duty of penance, requiring greater assistance of grace than the other. The third movement in the scale of penance is also given in St Paul, and it is this:

'God forbid that I should glory save in the cross of our Lord Jesus Christ, by whom the world is crucified to me and I to the world … and whosoever shall follow this rule, peace on them … I bear the marks of the Lord Jesus in my body.'[5]

To follow St Paul's rule, then, is to inherit peace. Could it indeed, in the light of our Lord's own words about the peace which He buys for us with His Passion, be otherwise? Total surrender to His Father's will, which is what the whole principle of penance amounts to, must inevitably be crowned by peace.

Peace is both the condition and the culmination. In heaven there will be no need for penance. There will be the plenitude of peace. Penance is our present concern; we can leave to God the question of its reward.

'That I may be found in Him, not having my justice which is of the law but that which is of the faith of Christ Jesus which is of God, justice in faith. That I may know Him and the power of His resurrection and *the fellowship of His sufferings being made conformable to His death*, if by any means I may attain to the resurrection which is from the dead.'[6] Here we have both the pattern of Christian penance and its justification: the model is Christ, the spirit is hope. Together the two ideals make up love.

---

4 Galatians 5:16, 18, 24-25
5 Galatians 6:14, 16-17
6 Philippians 3:9-11.

8
OBEDIENCE

BY penance a man aims at self-abnegation; by obedience he aims at self-annihilation.

By the vows of stability and conversion a monk renounces change of place and worldliness of life; by the vow of obedience he renounces the will that would choose change and the mind that is drawn by the world.

By poverty and chastity a man surrenders goods and heart; by obedience he surrenders self.

So stated, obedience sounds negative in purpose. A critic might say: 'Such obedience is doubtless heroic, but it is not very positive; give me something more constructive and less flattening.'

But love is positive enough, and in religious obedience the inspiration and end are love. Self-immolation and charity are here one thing. True sacrifice is positive, not negative.

If Christian obedience takes its character from Christ's obedience it can stand up to the charge of being flattening. 'I came not to do My own will but the will of Him who sent Me ... not My will but Thine be done.'[1]

The Christian who empties himself with Christ of his own will, becoming with Christ obedient unto death, has nothing to fear on

---

1   John 6:38, Matthew 25:39

the score of not being constructive. His will is actively engaged: it is uniting itself with the living will of Christ.

If our wills are the measure of ourselves—*'homines sunt voluntates'*, says St Augustine—then the surrender of the will to God in holy obedience is the surrender of all we have got, is the surrender of our whole selves.

The religious obedience which makes men selfless is different from the passive acquiescence which makes men spineless. Selfless in intention and desire, the religious mounts to the Father with the merits of Christ who was selfless in fact.

The obedience of Christ to His Father comprised in its act of complete subjection the perfection of order, truth, service, homage, love. His fulfilment of the Father's will was like the tree of Jesse, giving out new branches and bringing forth new fruit.

Christ's obedience is the condition of virtue. When the Father's will is finally and perfectly performed, Christ can say, *'Consummatum est'*, and it is time for His obedience to be crowned.

'Consummatum est': it is the Father's will, not His own, that has been fulfilled. There was nothing more that He could do or give, so He died.

'Yes,' you may say, 'but how does all this affect us? The submission of Christ to His Father is one thing, the submission which we owe to the Father—particularly when we have to express it through the hierarchic system of religious authority—is another. Is the connection between our obedience and Christ's purely mystical? Is His a symbol only, a type for our edification and meditation, or can we expect to find practical help in looking to His obedience for an example?'

Such a line of enquiry would not be concerned with Christ's obedience to the explicit word of the law. It is too obvious to need explanation that His observance of Jewish, and even of Roman, rule serves as a practical example to us in our attitude towards constituted authority. His submission to Joseph and Mary gives us an equally clear lead. The problem is a deeper one: how do we find our place in Christ's obedience, and how does His obedience give value to ours?

Suppose a man's father is defied by the servants of his own household. Suppose they continue to live at the expense of the master of the house, yet refuse to work or apologize or redress the harm done. What, assuming him to be devoted to his father, is the attitude of the son? Surely, he becomes even more loyal and obedient than he was before. His obedience is not only an example and a challenge to the others in the house, but a substitute. He obeys not only because he wants to please his father but because they do not. So, he is obeying not only for his own sake and for his father's sake, but for the sake of the rebels. His own perfection of obedience is to compensate for the disobedience of the rest.

The perfection of Christ's obedience to His Father's will, and the manner of it, brings His action into the closest relation to us. It means He is not only, by the fact of the Incarnation, a subject of the Father's authority, but a servant. 'Taking the form of a servant' He has become one among those who have refused service.

Not content with becoming a servant, He goes further than service and becomes a sacrifice. Going to the extreme limit of sacrifice, He is Himself the victim: the victim at once of divine love and human malice.

The Son, in vindication of the Father's honour and in reparation for man's dishonour, offers Himself on the altar to be consumed in the perfection of His obedience. We, the members of the household, are changed in Christ from being rebellious servants to adopted sons.

Not only are we made co-heirs with Christ, inheritors of the kingdom, but even in the kingdom of God on earth we are made co-operators with Christ in His work. 'Among all the gifts of God', says Dionysius the Areopagite, 'there is no gift more divine.'

If we who were the reprobate are now with Christ in reclaiming the reprobate, our fidelity to the pattern of Christ must be the closest possible: the obedience He followed must be ours, the love He gave must be ours, the sacrifice He made must be ours.

For the Christian, let alone for the religious, the obedience which Christ gave to the Father is a reality which makes all the difference to his service of God. Indeed, it is the reality on which the Christ-life and the prayer-life, and therefore particularly the religious life, are founded.

In telling the monk that 'by the labour of obedience you must return to Him from whom you departed by disobedience ... renouncing your own will and taking up the strong and bright armour of obedience to fight under the Lord Christ our true King', St Benedict indicates at once the theological, moral, and practical significance of religious obedience.

All obedience, Christ's and that of the religious, is the test and sign of love. 'If you keep My commandments,' said Christ on the last evening that He spent with the twelve, 'you shall abide in My love,' and He added immediately, 'as I also have kept My Father's commands and do abide in His love.' The connection between His act and His disciple's act is not accidental, it is essential.

It is Christ's obedience to His Father's commands that expresses His love—the love that He transmits to His disciples. Obedience is the guarantee of love, and the channel of love to others.

If to love and to be a Christian are ideally the same thing, then to be obedient and to be a Christian are ideally the same thing. If love and the religious vocation are the same thing, then obedience and the religious vocation are the same thing.

If Christ cannot allow an unrepentant rebel to exist in His body—any more than the Father can allow an unrepentant rebel to exist in heaven—then the first condition of membership must be unconditional surrender. If this is the case in regard to the subject and the Church, it is all the more so in regard to the religious and the religious life.

Where the Christian's obedience responds to the precept, the obedience of the religious, going beyond necessity, responds to the counsel. In either case the example, namely Christ, and the principle, namely submission of the will, are the same; it is the standard of observance and perfection that is different.

Whatever the degree of self-submission aspired to by the Christian in the world, self-immolation is the aim of the religious. St Jerome, commenting on the text 'if you will be perfect, follow Me', insists that to follow here means more than to walk in the same way, more even than to imitate: it means to surrender personal independence with the intention of being shaped by Christ and identified with Christ.

The shaping in Christ is effected for the religious in the environment to which his particular vocation has called him. It is not effected by it but in it. Perfection may not be looked for outside it. The shape of Christ's service, and therefore the shape of perfection, is defined for the religious by the rule under which he takes his vows, and by the will of the superior to whom he owes obedience.

Taking first the rule as a factor of influence in the formation of religious perfection, we can say of every religious order and congregation that its main purpose must be to bring the individual soul under the complete control of grace. Fidelity to his rule detaches a religious from the obstacles to grace and leaves his soul open to the free action of the Holy Ghost.

In one way or another the rule touches the religious at every moment of the day. No single point, however trivial in itself, falls outside the span of his obedience: with each duty, each recreation, each summons, the religious is being ordered about by the will of God. So far so good. But what happens when the religious interprets the order so literally as to hamper the free action of the Holy Ghost, and thus runs contrary to the will of God and to the whole purpose of the rule?

Clearly it is not obedience itself, the one thing which is meant to free the soul, that stifles the spirit. What stifles the spirit and turns obedience against itself is a false reading of the terms by which obedience is expressed. It is making a superstition of the forms in which obedience frames its demand.

For religious obedience to be fruitful the rule must be understood from the inside. There are many religious who preach about their rule, who have a great devotion to its text, who are exact in its outward performance, yet who completely miss its meaning.

Unless every now and again in the history of an order, or in the history of a community, a superior is raised up by God who can explain the inwardness of the rule, the spiritual energy is likely to be diverted into externalism, literalism, activism, and dissipation.

With the rule in his hands the religious should always be in a position to know what God wants of him. Where he may err is in judging how God wants it. If he is not to give a mistaken obedience he will need either clear light from God or a superior who guides him with the wisdom of the spirit.

'The more our judgment is enlightened by the values of faith,' writes Father Merton, 'the better we progress in ordinary obedience— and the better we can meet the rare necessity of blind obedience should the case arise. In any event, the prudent subject usually ought to understand each command in order to carry it out better. That is what superiors want.'

This doctrine in no way conflicts with the idea that so-called blind obedience is meritorious and heroic. Blind obedience is meritorious and heroic when the reason for the command given is not understood, when the superior withholds explanation, and when the execution of the command goes much against the grain. On such occasions the duty of the subject is to obey blindly, accepting the apparent unreason of the order and of the act as part of the obedience. But in the day-to-day practice of obedience what we need, as Father Merton points out, is not more blindness but more light.

We have, then, two factors to consider in our obedience: the rule and the authority that interprets it. So far as the rule goes, we stand to gain light upon its true spirit in the measure that we supernaturalize our fidelity to its letter. So far as authority goes, we gain grace and strength in the measure that we aim at obeying God in men.

Of the two, it is harder to give obedience to men than to the rule. In the case of the rule we have, or we think we have, an understanding of our holy founder's mind; in the case of superiors there is not always the same understanding, the same sense of affinity.

Just as it is easy to feel sympathy with Christ in the Gospel but not so easy to feel sympathy with Christ in the Church, so it is easy to take up a devotional attitude towards the rule and the founder while taking up a critical attitude towards superiors and their policy.

Whether God speaks by His revealed word, by the text of a religious rule, by the will of a superior, there is no distinction in right of authority. A monarch may give orders to his subjects in personal audience, by proclamation, over the air by broadcast, or through the medium of his government and ministers. It does not alter the obedience.

From obedience to grace and to God's will as manifested through the circumstances of life and the demands of the rule, the religious comes increasingly to appreciate the divine character of the authority that is vested in men. Fidelity to light produces fidelity to those who are so placed as to reflect the light.

By 'walking as children of the light' religious come more and more to see the meaning of our Lord's words about authority, come more and more to dread the least departure from respect and loyalty to their superiors.

Though the system of government in the religious life is hierarchic in constitution, it is in essence theocratic. If it ever degenerates into democratic or oligarchic rule it reduces the virtue of obedience almost to the secular state.

The principle and practice of religious obedience is concisely given by St Benedict in the fifth chapter of the Holy Rule. Here we see that the monk follows another's will because he cannot be sure of finding God in following his own.

True monks, says St Benedict, 'live not according to their own will nor pursue their own desires and pleasures, but, remaining in monasteries, live according to the command and direction of another, and want to have an abbot over them.' They *want* to have an abbot over them; they *choose* subjection.

A monk does not give obedience to his abbot either because he himself is obsequious by nature or because the abbot is a man after his own heart. He gives it because he knows that by being under someone else he is more directly under God.

Freed from the yoke of self, the monk, bound by the will of another which denotes for him the will of God, gives a service which is joyous, spontaneous, and prompt. Monastic obedience according to the mind of St Benedict is pleasing to God and men 'if what is commanded be not done in fear, or haltingly, coldly, with murmuring or with an answer that shows unwillingness.'

The promptitude insisted upon in Benedictine obedience springs from the unencumbered heart, the heart which, to quote from St Benedict's fourth chapter, 'desires life everlasting with spiritual thirst, that prefers nothing to the love of Christ, and that knows for certain that God is our witness everywhere.'

It would hardly be possible for a monk to be on the alert to obey outwardly unless interiorly his will was equally alert to respond to grace. Alacrity in meeting the summons of obedience is the surest sign that the will is not tied down by anything: instinctively the soul is answering to the good.

Some are by temperament more hesitating than others. For these it is not so easy to live up to St Benedict's ideal as it is for the naturally impetuous. To the monk who is spontaneous and generous by nature, who is precipitous in his decisions, the sudden call of obedience is stimulating. To him it is no great sacrifice to 'leave unfinished what he is about, and with the speedy foot of obedience follow by deeds the voice of him who commands'; but for the more reflex monk such promptitude may call for heroism. It is for this latter monk to see in St Benedict's words an inner meaning which will spur him to a quicker outward fulfilment: he is to leave his doubts and mental discussions unresolved, and with swift act of faith follow by deeds the human voice of Him who commands in the name of love.

Nor is it only St Benedict who makes such a point of this hair-trigger obedience. '*Obedientia reddit promptam voluntatem hominis,*' says St Thomas, '*ad implendum voluntatem alterius.*'[2] In another place the same doctor teaches that it springs from the reverence which the soul has for the one commanding. If religious really saw God in their superiors, this reverence would be assured, and there would never be any question of obedience being delayed for an instant.

The reason why St Benedict comes out so strongly against murmuring is not only because it is an evil in itself, and one that spreads quickly in a community; the reason is also because murmuring is the unmistakable sign that the murmurer is not seeing Christ in his abbot. Murmuring in a monk is an admission that an essential purport of the Holy Rule has passed him by.

The monk who murmurs against either a superior or a command given by a superior or a policy with which he disagrees, is going back on that submission of the will which is the necessary condition of the religious life. If 'obedience is the way that leads to God', he is turning

---

2 Obedience renders the will of a man prompt to fulfil the will of another

round and going in the wrong direction.

A monk may imagine that he is inspired with the loftiest motives in his criticism, may say that he criticizes quite without bitterness, may protest that there is nothing personal in his attacks, may feel no guilt at having murmured. He is a murmurer and stands condemned as such by St Benedict. He is seeing the man in the superior and not God; he is seeing a policy which he dislikes and not the will of God; he is looking at the material thing ordered instead of at the supernatural thing which it signifies. He is admitting that he lacks faith.

'Above all things take heed that there be no murmuring, by word or sign, upon any occasion whatsoever.' Commenting on St Benedict's strictures, Abbot Delatte says that 'as in St Benedict's eyes monastic peace is a benefit which surpasses all others, so murmuring seems to him the worst of evils.'

Referring back to the three conceptions of peace noted earlier, the Greek, the Roman, and the Hebrew, we see now that St Benedict's understanding of obedience secures the best elements of each. Dependence upon authority as having the sanction of God promotes the Athenian calm and balance; complete subjection to rule and abbot secures in the community the order which makes for peace; the view that peace is a grace which may not be threatened by murmuring, listlessness in God's service, rebellious thought, embodies the peace of the Jews.

In obedience a monk finds not only peace but safety from the spirit of the world. Each time he transgresses he edges closer to the line which he crossed for good when he came into the monastery. When a monk vows obedience he begins a new life in the spirit. As explicitly as in the case of his vow to convert himself from the manners of the world he pledges himself to a way of faith. It is understandable that those who begin in the flesh should be blind enough to end in the flesh, but it is a tragedy that those who begin in the spirit should be blind enough to end in the flesh.

When we think of sins against religious obedience we think of open resistances and downright refusals. We forget that to obey with an air of martyrdom designed to attract the superior's attention, with a plan to canvass the sympathy of others, with the intention of appealing to higher authority if there should be the least grounds for expecting a favourable judgment, is also to act contrary to obedience. It would probably be blackmail as well.

Take it one stage further. Obedience is imperfect where there is a suspicion of superiors, where there is a readiness to question the wisdom of their decisions; where guarantees of good faith are expected of superiors before proceeding to fulfil their commands.

If the monk waits till he can see what is going on in the mind of his abbot and can approve it, he may have to wait for ever before he obeys him.

If the monk obeys only when he judges his abbot to be as monastically orientated as himself, he is not being obedient to God in his abbot but to a projection of himself in his abbot.

If the monk withholds his obedience until he is sure that his abbot is as much St Benedict's idea of an abbot as he himself is St Benedict's idea of a monk, he has missed both monasticism and St Benedict altogether.

Let the monk obey first, and then he will see all that he needs to see about monasticism: namely, that its strength lies in the ordering of obedience. If promptitude in obedience is the sign of love in the heart of the monk, it is also a condition of light upon the essential nature of the monastic life.

For a monk to be selective in his obedience, choosing only the points of the Holy Rule that suit him and limiting his response to superiors according to his monastic or even interior attraction, is virtually to rewrite the Rule in his own name. It is to establish himself as a father founder; it is to constitute himself abbot over a community of one.

'If we obey one precept and not another,' says the greatest monastic genius since St Benedict, 'the coin of our obedience is broken, and Christ will not accept it.' St Bernard develops his simile with strong words: 'If we make a feint of obeying under the master's eye, while murmuring secretly, our coin is debased; there is lead in it, all is not silver, we are paying in false talents. Therein lies our iniquity. We defraud, but it is under God's eye. Now God is not mocked.'

Another way in which we can present counterfeit coin is to mint our currency under cover of dispensations and permissions. It is a mistake to think that we can 'regularize' our imperfect obedience by the act of extracting a superior's consent. If our obedience is imperfect, the remedy lies not in permissions but in perfecting our obedience.

An act that is sanctioned by a superior is not necessarily sanctified by the superior's act. In the same way, to explain to a superior afterwards that we have transgressed, even though we ask pardon on our knees and beg a penance, is not to turn a disobedience into an obedience.

A monk may be exact in getting every sort of permission, but if he does so as a backstairs way of evading obedience his permissions are more a superstition than an observance of religious rule and custom.

When a monk has got himself dispensed from the duties which he finds irksome, how much obedience will be left? His abbot may be either edified or irritated by his constantly coming to ask for permission, but in God's sight how much is there in all this of true obedience?

It may cost the monk a good deal in the way of humiliation to be constantly asking for permissions. So much the better: mortification is good for all of us. But this, as regards obedience, is not the point. The point is, does his virtue of obedience allow him to be so often dispensed?

Thus, in the name of obedience we can find ourselves shuffling out of obedience—as in the name of obedience we can find ourselves shuffling out of prayer and penance and even charity. There seem to be no lengths to which self-deception cannot go.

But self-deception can take us the other way too. It is as false to the principle of obedience to be rigorist as to be lax. Thus, we must admit, however exalted our ideal, that there will be occasions when it is necessary, when it is even a duty, for the monk to ask for dispensations. In the same way there will be occasions when it is necessary and a duty to waive personal loyalty in the correction of an abuse. Neither justifiable dispensation nor conscientious complaint can offend against obedience.

The way to get grace in these twilight cases is not to ask, 'Am I justified in asking to be relieved of this, to be absented from that?' The surer way is to deepen one's love of obedience, and in the light of this love there will be not the least desire to ask for unnecessary dispensations. 'Am I justified... dare I?' will not come up: to be dispensed without reason would cause acute distress.

By the same token the question is not, 'Am I murmuring ... may I legitimately make representations about this abuse?' The question is, 'Do I really love obedience?' If I do, any steps I take towards correcting abuses will be taken with dread and with deep humility, and only because my conscience forces me to take them.

'My meat is to do the will of Him who sent Me, and to accomplish the task He gave Me to do.' This is the word by which obedience lives. It means that one work is not chosen in preference to another, one work done languidly and another with zest, one work finished and another left off before the end.

It means that obedience makes holy the meanest work and that disobedience makes mean the holiest. Short prayers under obedience are more pleasing to God than long prayers made independently of obedience, small penances with the blessing of authority are more pleasing to God than heroic penances without. Obedience insures not only that all things come to us from God, but that all things go back again to God from us.

We are to be, St Peter tells us, 'as children of obedience, not fashioned according to the former desires of your ignorance but according to Him that called you.'[3] To be a child of obedience must mean that we grow up in the virtue and not only in the vow. We aim at perfecting the virtue, not merely at fulfilling the vow.

Men write this and that about obedience, teach this and that in retreats and community chapters, but when you work it all down to a formula you find that charity embraces every article of the doctrine. Love alone teaches the fulness of obedience, obedience alone proves the fulness of love.

'The concern of discipline is love,' says the book of Wisdom, 'and love is the keeping of her laws: and the keeping of her laws is the firm

---

3   1 Peter 1:14

foundation of incorruption: and incorruption brings near to God.'[4] St John says it even more simply: 'He who keepeth His word, in him in very deed the charity of God is perfected.'[5]

---

4   Wisdom 6:19
5   1 John 2:5

BOOK II
THE YOKE OF PRAYER

1
INDIVIDUAL PRAYER

SINCE prayer is the act which draws together and expresses the relations of the soul with God, it is the climax to which all the other exercises of the religious life are directed. The fact that it is a daily, even hourly, climax makes its performance all the more difficult: there is nothing that so familiarizes a climax as the repeated effort of prayer.

'The whole scope of monastic life and its highest perfection', says Cassian, 'consists in a constant and uninterrupted perseverance in prayer, and in preserving, as far as human frailty will permit, peace of soul and purity of heart. The whole edifice of the virtues is raised only to attain the perfection of prayer, and if it be not crowned with prayer which unites and binds all the parts together it will be neither solid nor lasting.'

According to Cassian, then, prayer and the virtues are complementary: without the virtues it is impossible to reach the perfection of prayer, and without the practice of prayer the virtues are hindered in their full development. Since we have treated of some monastic virtues in the first section of this book, and since we shall be treating of others in the third, we can confine the present section to the question of prayer.

Just as prayer is the prepared environment of the religious vows and virtues, faith is the prepared environment of prayer. It is faith that moves the will to prepare.

When the will, freely operating in faith, moves the soul to give worship to God, there is already the response to grace: prayer has begun. *'Domine, inclina caelos tuos et descende.'*[1] By making room for God whom it knows by faith, the will is welcoming God who is already present in fact.

The human will when freely choosing to pray is the area in which the meeting between God and the soul—and ultimately the full union of God and the soul—takes place. It is the enclave, silent and empty and waiting, in which the mystical life is born.

St Augustine says of man's response to God in prayer that it is one of those things where God does all and the soul does all, and that it is no good trying to see where the one leaves off and the other begins. It is to man's free will that God freely offers Himself, and it is man's free will that chooses between filling up the soul with false desires or else emptying it and receiving the fulness of love. The mystery of free will is the mystery of love.

Allowing that the choice is made according to grace and that the human personality wishes to correspond with the divine, the first step is made: the interior life has begun. Like a diver for pearls, the soul that was naked and poverty-stricken one minute is rich beyond measuring the next.

Wanting now to go out to God in love and worship, the soul learns that though the conditions of the relationship are in God's hands, the modes of expression are in its own. Thus, God is found to define the stages of the soul's progress while allowing the soul to choose, in the light of grace, the forms of converse.

God arranges by what way the soul is to be guided; the soul decides by what way to communicate with Him on the journey. God draws the soul to this or that articulation of prayer; the soul is left to arrange which articulation to use, and when.

It is like an artist being left to choose his medium. He has been

---

[1] 'O Lord, incline your heavens and descend.' — Ps. 143:5

provided with a certain vision and a certain creative faculty: will he realize these gifts in stone or wood, in watercolour or oil, in etching or pen? Whichever he chooses, and he may choose each of them at one time or another, it is someone else who decides when he is qualified and who confers his awards.

In getting into touch with God by prayer the soul has a variety of prayer-expressions at its disposal. At one time a devotional form may be employed, at another a liturgical, or a discursive, or a wordless form. Of the two main channels of communication supplied by grace to man—the one private and interior, the other public and vocal—the liturgical and corporate prayer of the Church is objectively superior in dignity and merit. But where there is greater purity of heart in the unofficial worship that goes up from individual souls—in other words, where the subjective element is taken as the grounds for judgment—it may well happen that solitary prayer surpasses in value the prayer given socially in the choir.

The whole thing depends upon love. The Divine Office has the weight of authority, tradition, its place in the prayer that is given by the blessed in heaven, and its altogether comprehensive character to recommend it before God. But if it is without love it has no force. Private prayer has on its side spontaneity, flexibility, the fact that it is the immediate vehicle of emotions felt here and now by a particular person, and the quality of being able to express itself without words. But, again, if it is without love, it is a waste of time.

Since every prayer, whether a chanted psalm or a silent turning of the soul to God in love, is judged on its own merits, and since it is God alone who can be the judge, it is idle to claim first place for either liturgical or interior prayer. Each leans on the other, fulfils and verifies the other.

But since normally it is mental prayer that ministers to and perfects liturgical prayer rather than the other way about, it will here be discussed first. Not that the function of mental prayer is to train the mind for the work of giving solemn worship to God—as a young courtier would have to be trained before attendance at the throne—but that *in* giving solemn worship to God the disposition is created by mental prayer.

There is this, however, to be noted about mental prayer: in playing a subordinate role it comes first, but being the stuff of mysticism it also comes last. It prepares for and purifies liturgical prayer; and then eventually crowns it.

Prayer should not be to the religious the difficulty that it is often made out to be, and that to the layman it undoubtedly must be. The layman has to snatch time for prayer at irregular intervals when and where he can; he comes to prayer handicapped by distractions and goes from it to distractions; he is never quite sure that other duties do not require of him the sacrifice of his prayer; he has probably not been trained in prayer, so does not know what to expect; nor has he time to study the standard works.

As against this the religious has the whole framework of the religious life to help him. His rule, his timetable, his spiritual reading, his training, his study: everything points in the one direction, stressing the need and making possible the practice. Not merely making possible the practice, but making desirable the practice.

When the religious goes to prayer he may go from a timetable as crowded as that of the layman's, but at least he does not labour under the distracting doubt about whether or not he should be coming to prayer at all. He knows that his whole life is meant to be a prayer and that it can never be this unless he secures set times for serious, concentrated, uninterrupted mental prayer. Moreover, they must be the best times, not the worst, and spaced out regularly.

Each order has its own regulations about the amount of time to be given to mental prayer, and most communities have in addition customs of their own which act as further guarantees. It can hardly be going against the letter of any religious rule, or against the spirit of any religious house, to claim that not less than an hour a day should be devoted to this strictly interior exercise. If no more than an hour can be spared from the day, it

is best to make half an hour's mental prayer in the morning and another half-hour in the evening.

This prayer should be made in relation to other duties and not wedged in at intervals when there is nothing much else going on. It is not less important than other works but more. The attitude should not be: 'My work is given to me by God and I must bring into it what prayer I can so as to perfect it', but rather: 'My prayer is given to me by God as my main work, and the way in which I handle the active side of my life will show whether or not I am praying as much as God wants.'

Nor should these set hours or half-hours be combined with anything else—with taking exercise, for instance, or resting in a chair after manual labour. Mental prayer is not a dreamy way of spending pious time. To bring intimate converse with God into competition with an open-air study of flowers, of the habits of birds, of architectural detail is to dissipate the impulse. It is also, looked at another way, an irreverence.[2]

The obvious exception to this exclusiveness is the combining of mental prayer and hearing—even, for those who can manage it, serving—Mass. Here we are not trying to do two things at once: we are trying to do one thing better.

Praying for half an hour at and with the Mass, we not only benefit by the graces which flow immediately from the infinite merits of Christ's sacrifice, but we have as an anchorage to our attention the Mass's actions, symbols, prayers. There could be no better background to prayer: the Mass provides its foundation and inspiration. But we must follow the interior attraction of grace in this; we should not feel obliged, thinking that otherwise we are missing grace, to combine our time of mental prayer with that of hearing Mass. This would be a scruple.

---

2 This is not to exclude souls from making their stipulated recollections out of doors—still less of course is it meant to discourage even the closest converse with God apart from set prayer times—but only to deprecate the idea that because one needs to take more exercise one might as well make mental prayer subservient to this end. Souls who find that they can pray better in the open should, if their regulations allow, follow the attraction. Sometimes it is the only way to keep awake. Many of the saints preferred praying out of doors. Some religious founders expressly allow for it. Our Lord prayed out of doors, and that settles it. The disparagement suggested above is not directed against praying out of doors (see below, 131, where the question of recollection and the practice of the presence of God is considered) but against prejudicing prayer by trying to do two things at once. Clearly, we should try to pray everywhere.

Again, it would be a mistake to argue from what has been said either that singing in choir during a High Mass could be mental prayer, or that, because they provided anchorage to attention and were sources of inspiration, such things as meditative reading, stations of the cross, Benediction, or the slow recitation of the rosary could be 'counted' as mental prayer. Nothing counts as mental prayer but mental prayer.

It is true that in the early days our fathers in religion knew no fixed times for mental prayer. But they seem nevertheless to have practised it. St Benedict nowhere insists in the Holy Rule on mental prayer as a separate exercise. But we know from what St Gregory says in the second book of the Dialogues that he practised it. 'Being diligent in watching, and making his prayer about midnight' St Benedict is described as experiencing a mystical transport of a high order: 'the whole world was represented to his eyes in one single ray of light ... bright and resplendent.' In another place the saint is spoken of as 'praying for a long time', and from the context it looks as though the prayer lasted all night. On another occasion he is found 'in his cell at his prayers'.

From the Holy Rule all we can get on the subject of private prayer is this: 'Not for our much speaking but for our purity of heart and tears of compunction shall we be heard. Our prayer ought therefore to be short and pure, unless perhaps prolonged by the inspiration of grace... if anyone desire to pray in private let him come in simply and pray, not with a loud voice but with tears and fervour of heart.' The monk 'who perchance wishes to pray by himself' is instructed to stay behind when the others have gone out of the oratory after the Divine Office.

Is this a meagre treatment of the subject? Not when you consider the drift of St Benedict's thought, and the method which he employs in regard to other aspects of the monk's life. He knows that the monk who really wants God will want to pray on his own. The formal prayer of the community will not be enough, and will only stimulate a desire for more.

In shaping the spirits of his monks, St Benedict holds to a uniform principle: care for nothing more than Christ, and the means of uniting yourself with Him must follow. We have seen this principle at work in the case of obedience, penance, poverty, and turning from the world. Love God, and you will find yourself loving to do the things that lead to love.

Does this mean that if I love God I must also love prayer? Is it really only one love?—or if it is two, does one act as the measure of the other? I know that prayer is at once the expression of love and the means of attaining to love … yet, if I am honest, dare I say that in practice I love praying?

Surely there is a distinction between loving prayer and loving to pray. We may not like it, but if we love we go to it with desire. For months our prayer may be the greatest weariness, may even be a suffering; but love drives us to it. The incentive is not fear, or routine, or human respect; it is love. It is not a sensible but a secret love: it is the obscure desire to learn love. There is nothing wrong with this kind of love, this kind of prayer.

'With desire I have desired to eat this pasch with you before I suffer.'[3] Christ did not enjoy looking forward to His Passion. In a sense the whole of His life was a spun-out pasch, a rehearsal of suffering. But because He loved His Father's will and His disciples, He desired to eat it before the actual summons to pain and death.

'If it be possible let this chalice pass from Me.'[4] But because He loved the Father's will and His disciples, He loved to drain it.

The more a religious gives himself to the work of interior prayer, the more directly does Christ reproduce Himself in his life and operate through his hands. 'I live, now not I, but Christ lives in me.'[5] Whether prayer delights or disgusts me is immaterial. What do I matter anyway? Prayer delights God, and this should be enough for me. For all I know it may delight Him in proportion as it disgusts me; in which case I should be glad to suffer the disgust.

My work for souls, my progress in the virtues, the good I derive from the sacraments, my religious sense and the deepening of my understanding of the vows: all this depends upon the degree to which I 'walk in Christ', to which I 'put on Christ'. Prayer makes actual to

---

3   Luke 22:15
4   Matthew 26:39
5   Galatians 2:20

me the reality of Christ in my soul; prayer opens out before me the implications.

If I were a saint, the whole horizon would be filled with Christ. Everything about me would speak to me of Christ. I would not have to look for Him in others: love would reveal Him. He is there all the time, only my lack of love, of prayer, of faith has made me blind.

I would not have to worry about this or that work taking me from prayer. Nor would I have to worry about this or that prayer taking me from work. All would be one in love, in Christ. 'Is he silent?' it was said of St Hugh, Abbot of Cluny, 'then it is because he is always with the Lord. Does he speak? then it is in the Lord and about the Lord that he speaks.'

It has been suggested above that if prayer can in any way be held to constitute the soul's essential life, at least one hour in the twenty-four will be needed for mental prayer—the act which focuses and intensifies the prayer activity which goes on outside that hour. But individual souls will be drawn to spend longer time than this in the exercise. They will want, particularly in the early stages and again in the most advanced, to spend every available minute praying interiorly to God.

Nor does this conflict with St Benedict's idea that length should be sacrificed to purity and compunction: he covers himself, it must be remembered, with the condition 'unless prolonged by the inspiration of divine grace'. The movement behind the whole activity of prayer is divine grace, and divine grace very frequently urges the soul to prolong these recollections.

St Augustine, in a letter reassuring his spiritual daughter Proba, says on this point: 'It is neither wrong nor unprofitable to spend much time in praying provided there be leisure for this without hindering other good and necessary works, although even in the doing of these we ought, by fostering holy desire, to pray without ceasing. For to spend a long time in prayer is not, as some think, the same thing as to pray with much speaking. Multiplied words are one thing, long-continued desire is another. For even of the Lord Himself it is written that He continued all night in prayer, and that His prayer was more prolonged when He was in an agony.'

So, despite the lack of time-tabled mental prayer in the lives of the early saints, mystics, monks and nuns, we can conclude that the place which it occupies in the lives of modern religious was not wholly supplied by the greater abstraction enjoyed by our ancestors in religion.

Perhaps we make too much of the contrast between our own distracting circumstances and the simpler setting of the ancients. Perhaps we press its implications too far, and so make too many excuses for ourselves. Perhaps it would be better if, by giving greater stress to the values stressed by the ancients, we sought to reduce the differences. Psychologically and spiritually, we have much in common; it is in religious spirit that there seems to have been a decline.

Be this as it may, the only way to keep vivid the Christ-life which we know in faith is to reproduce it as nearly as we can in love and prayer. No service, whether of God or of man, can be faithfully kept up where the channel of communication is narrowed to necessity. Still less, on those terms, can such service be perfected.

Prayer in the life of the religious is meant to be a state, and states cannot be maintained without fidelity to their specific acts.

The specific act of prayer is not talking or writing about it; it is not even speculating about it in solitude, not kneeling before the Blessed Sacrament vaguely wishing, not mounting into the skies of the imagination in flight from terrestrial and ugly reality. The specific act of prayer is loving—wanting to love—God.

The saints knew no other specific act than this. It was the specific act of our Lady's prayer. If prayer and love of God are virtually convertible terms, it means that there cannot be an increase in love where there is deficiency in prayer. If the plenitude of the one is aimed at, a bare sufficiency of the other will not do. I can no more attain to a maximum of love on a minimum of prayer than I can attain to the perfection of prayer when that which gives it life is selfish or imperfect.

In the actual pursuit of prayer, I shall be overwhelmed at times by the sense of futility and defeat. I shall feel that of all the works which I have tried to do for God, the work of private, interior, loving attention to Him has been the most signal failure. Nothing has seemed to waste more time, nothing has seemed to bear less fruit.

Yet if I go on wanting to give Him glory, what is there to show that

He is not getting it? Certainly, my lack of measurable success is no proof. 'To find God is to seek Him without ceasing,' says St Gregory of Nyssa; 'indeed it is not one thing to seek Him and another to find Him. The fruit of our search is to seek Him still more. The desire of the soul is fulfilled by the very fact that it becomes insatiable, for to see God is to desire Him without limit.'

2

LITURGICAL PRAYER

THE liturgy can be considered from various angles—historical, symbolical, ceremonial, aesthetic, musical, and so on—each of which has its bearing upon the angle to be considered here. Here we consider the liturgy from the contemplative angle: the *Opus Dei* as fulfilled contemplatively and monastically in choir.

If other aspects of the liturgy help to promote prayer at the Divine Office, the more they are studied the better. If they distract from such prayer, it means they are either being misunderstood or over-emphasized, and should be corrected.

The best way to correct faults of wrong emphasis is not directly, by disposing of the particular liturgical form which is getting too much attention, but indirectly, by seeing to the element of recollection and contemplation which is not getting enough attention.

What prevents the contemplative rendering of the Divine Office is not the prominence given to singing and ceremonies, but the prominence not given to contemplation.

If a religious is neglectful of the prayer which he offers to God out of choir, he is not likely to advance in the prayer which God offers to him in it.

Unless the prayer which the Divine Office presents to the soul finds a corresponding activity in the soul itself, the full liturgical prayer is incomplete.

Thus, a monk's union with God at other times will condition his union with God during the Divine Office. And the Divine Office in turn unites him more closely to God in his private prayer. But though the Divine Office may create interior dispositions for prayer, it does not take the place of them.

The liturgy does not exist to save souls the trouble of praying.

The immanence of God which the Divine Office impresses upon the soul becomes an abiding reality only if the soul goes out to meet it. When lived with, it in turn disposes the soul for further light to be derived through the Divine Office. But though the Divine Office impresses God's power and presence, it does not dispense the soul from learning about them.

The liturgy was not invented as a short cut to the knowledge of God's attributes.

In the degree to which a religious adapts his spirituality to the liturgical form, he will find that both in choir and out he comes to see new and deeper implications in the wording of the psalms. When actually following the lessons, prayers, chapters, hymns and antiphons he will wonder why their inner significance has never struck him before.

Nevertheless, the liturgy has not been drawn up for the sake of explaining texts.

What then is the essential work of the liturgy? If its primary purpose is neither to dispose, to instruct, nor explain, what is there left that it can do for the soul?

Perhaps the confusion lies in assuming that the liturgy's essential work is related primarily to the soul and not to God. The liturgy, as we shall see, does much for the soul. In some cases it may be said to do everything. But the purpose of the liturgy is realized in heaven rather than on earth.

In case this should seem to belittle the effect as it concerns man, we know that most choir-religious are shaped in their spirituality by the Divine Office. Their development in the theological virtues and the gifts of the Holy Ghost, their relations in community, their practical judgment and monastic outlook: all take their colour and find their impulse from the liturgical life.

Even leaving aside the most sacred factor in the liturgy, namely the sacramental factor at the centre of which is the Mass itself, the *Opus Dei* on its own merits is formative, enlightening, sanctifying. But over and above all this the first purpose of the liturgy is to give glory to God.

The distinction must therefore be made between the objective act and the subjective disposition and effect. The Divine Office is a fact of worship, an activity which in itself is pleasing to God. The Divine Office is also the movement of the individual mind and heart.

In all prayer, not only in the Divine Office, the two elements are present: God is the object of the soul's desire, the soul's desire is the subject or term of departure. In all prayer, not only in the Divine Office, the tendency is to become so interested in the subjective operation as to forget the objective intention, to think too much about what the soul is getting out of it and not enough about what God is getting out of it.

Instinctively man values a thing by the effect it has upon him, by his own response to it. His emotions are, after all, his natural screen of reference. His reason and his experience may tell him that a wiser plan would be to judge the thing on its intrinsic merit; but he will still go on judging from his own point of view. If he is a man with any religion his reason and faith will tell him that things are valuable only for the value that they possess in the sight of God; but he will still, unless he makes a great point of thinking twice before he judges, value things according to their effect upon himself.

The Divine Office is a thing done. It has a value quite apart from the value which it has for me. To see the whole of this thing done by religious in choir, to see it in its objective and subjective connotation, I shall need to see it from God's point of view.

The implications of this are many. One encouraging conclusion which may be drawn from the argument is that it should not be difficult for me to judge the value of the part I take in the Divine Office. More easily than in the case of my private prayer I can detach myself from my tortuous self-investigations and see the thing objectively from above.

I can, it is true, deceive myself about that aspect of my liturgical prayer which concerns my interior dispositions. But now my interior dispositions are only half the story, not the whole. The part that is the other half is known to me: I can be certain that the Divine Office is giving glory to God, and that whatever my own shortcomings in the matter it is valuable in its own right.

The reason for the existence of the liturgy then, absolutely speaking, is God. The act performed by man, at the direction of the Church, is good. It is good not only because it has been handed down by tradition, because it has been beautified by art, because the saints have taken part in it and hallowed it: it is good on its own, *fine operis*,[1] because it regards God alone and because it is something which God wants done.

The Mass, the very heart of the liturgy, is valuable above all other acts that can be performed on earth precisely because, lifted out of the sphere where the mental attitude of the person performing it is the qualifying factor, it belongs to an order where the sole qualification is in the mind of God and is here entirely and absolutely acceptable.

All other works which man may give to God—from objectively neutral ones which he sanctifies by fulfilling them with a supernatural intention to directly sanctifying works such as he performs when fulfilling the beatitudes—are supernaturally pleasing to God because of the love which enters into them, *finis operantis*.[2] The Mass *is* love.

Monastic choirs, with their conventual Mass to set the rhythm of the day, are thus amplifiers of God's word and of God's love. It is significant that the terms used in traditional writing with regard to the Divine Office are those used also in connection with the Mass. Worship in choir is sacrifice, homage, gratitude, rendering of the common debt, an expression of united love.

Each separate hour of the Divine Office is an echo of the Mass. The Office finds its climax and its impulse in the Mass. As the Mass does not depend upon the devotion of the celebrant, so the Divine Office does not depend upon the devotion of the choir-religious.

The words *Opus Dei* do not refer only to the work which we do for

---

1 By the end of the work itself.
2 The end of the one working.

God in choir; they refer also, and more comprehensively, to what He does for us. There is little enough that we can do, beyond keeping the rubrics and trying to attend, but when it comes to trying to estimate the action of God upon the soul in choir we are in a world of imponderables.

In the Divine Office God admits man, as He does in the Mass, to His own prayer—the prayer that passes between the Persons of the Blessed Trinity. The *Gloria Patri* at the end of each psalm should remind us of this. We do not bow at the antiphon which gives us the cue or the mood: we bow at the *Gloria Patri* which gives us the vibration of a divine prayer. The liturgy that is observed by the blessed in heaven is contained in this doxology that we repeat on earth.

Is it too far-fetched to give to St Benedict's *'nihil Operi Dei praeponatur'*[3] an interpretation which is not the immediate one, and to say that nothing *can* take precedence of the *Opus Dei*? Even to give the ordinary meaning to the words, admitting that St Benedict wanted his monks to rank choir attendance higher than any other duty, is to carry an attitude far: we are left in no doubt as to the Benedictine understanding of liturgical prayer.

'Let nothing be preferred to the *Opus Dei*.' Whether you take it as meaning that the Divine Office is in fact the most important thing that can be done, or whether you look on it simply as a straightforward injunction, it is the text on which the monk bases his spirituality. His monasticism grows out of this idea, and increasingly comes to grow round it. The Divine Office is the pivot of the monk's life.

The Divine Office does not exclude other works; it is simply given pride of place. The question as to whether or not other works are to be undertaken is decided in the light of its primary importance. Not every work is compatible with regular attendance in choir, and the more often a work takes the monk away from his main duty the more clear must be the obedience which demands it.

Nothing could be further from the mind of St Benedict than a habitual exemption from the work of God on the plea of work for souls. The Divine Office is work for souls. If the Holy Spirit calls a man to

---

3 Let nothing be placed before the Work of God.

the service of liturgical prayer, He is, in the terms of the vocation, not calling him to the service of anything that militates against that first call. The monk can, without disloyalty to Christian obligation, resist the pull which drags him to the works of the apostle. Indeed, if he is to be a good monk and a good Christian *and a good apostle*, he must resist it.

Councils and Popes have repeatedly laid down that the vocation to the choir makes as important a contribution to the life of the mystical body as the vocation to care for the sick and to preach to the heathen. Once granted that a soul has been given this vocation, it must be obedience alone that sends him out to work for others.

In his choir-stall he is safe. In his choir-stall he is being what he is meant to be. In the name of the whole Christian family to which he belongs, he is offering homage and reparation. With Christ he is a mediator, a petitioner, a representative. He may even, if he is admitted far enough into the mystery of Christ praying through the liturgy, be a victim.

When it is said of the religious that he is safe and at home in his choir, it is not suggested that he is cosy. The monk does not wrap himself up in his cowl when he chants the canonical hours and forget his brethren in the world who are engaged in a more active warfare. He fights, but at a different level of reality.

The Church, with centuries of experience behind her, does not give her blessing to a life which is hindering her own life. She is not, as if with motherly concern, indulging certain favoured ones among her children and letting them live snug and comfortable. Nor is she keeping alive a fancy conceived by the fathers of the desert, treasuring for the sake of tradition the worn-out habit of the cenobitical life.

The Church knows what she is about, and in making every effort to encourage vocations to the monastic life and to the choir she is fostering the common life of charity within herself. It is the Bride of Christ seeing to it that the works of the members are duly distributed.

This being so, it puts a heavy responsibility upon the monastic orders and upon individual monks. If it is thus that we stand in relation to the world and to God, how dare we ever leave our choirs at all? How, when we are in them, do we dare to forget our obligation?

Is it possible that we should suffer distractions as we do in our private prayer, that we should tire, get irritable, not care?

The best person to answer these questions, and he does so as much by his life as by his teaching, is St Bernard. While consistently proclaiming that 'the function of the monk is to weep and not to teach', he nevertheless allowed that there were occasions when it might be God's will for the monk to engage in outward works, and that if this were so 'he must sacrifice his withdrawn life in order to give life to others'. When the occasion came up in his own life, this is exactly what he did.

From St Bernard's sermons on the Canticle we know that for the soul ordered in charity the works of the contemplative life are valued before all other. The *'nihil Operi Dei praeponatur'* will be subscribed to instinctively. But though union with God in contemplation and in choir is chosen by the soul *ordo affectualis*, union with God's will in works of charity and obedience may have to be chosen by the soul *ordo actualis*.[4]

We may not use contemplation as a stick with which to beat action. Nor, once forced into the way of action, may we persuade ourselves that action is the better.

'We must remember', writes Father Merton commenting on St Bernard's Canticle sermons, 'that activity cannot legitimately claim *all* our time and all our energies. This will enable us to avoid the pitfalls of activism, and to seize all the opportunities for contemplation and solitude that God puts in our way.'

So, it comes to this, that if there is to be work for souls in the life of the monk it must be a kind that is monastic—bound up with, and not divorced from, the liturgy. Essentially the monk's apostolate is contemplative; only accidentally may it be active and extra-claustral.

All the more need then that the sheltered life be prevented from being a sterile life. Freed from so many external commitments the monk must use his time well. If the Divine Office is all he has got as a medium for conveying his zeal for souls he must give to it at least what the preacher gives to his work of preaching, what the missioner gives to his teaching and baptizing.

---

4 In the affectual order; in the actual order.

There is the danger of sitting in choir as a passenger, leaving the singing and the psalmody to do the whole thing. Yes, taking part in the sounds made and the movements required, but swimming with the current instead of taking an active and intelligent part. '*Psallite sapienter*', St Benedict quotes from the forty-sixth psalm.[5] We should so sing in choir, he tells us in the same nineteenth chapter, that mind and voice are in accord.

To 'sing His praises with understanding' in the terms of the psalm is not to sing as a scholar; it is rather to sing as a student.

To let mind and voice accord together in their ascent to Truth and Wisdom is an action which invites a return of knowledge and grace out of all proportion to the natural effort. Following with the brain and lips is only the first response to grace, but it is a necessary one. The raising of the mind and heart comes next, and this is even more rewarding to the soul.

'From where did the holy doctors of the early ages and the venerable patriarchs of the desert acquire their spiritual knowledge and tender devotion?' asks Dom Gueranger. 'It was from those long hours of psalmody during which truth, simple yet manifold, unceasingly passed before the eyes of their souls, filling those souls with streams of light and love.'

Readiness to learn from the liturgy as well as readiness to perfect ourselves in its performance is a condition which makes demands upon our attention. It is as well that the central act of our day as monks should make demands of us.

What other demands does it make? If the sole hardship entailed is keeping awake, we are hardly justified in claiming for it the title of sacrifice. That it is a sacrifice of praise we have already seen, that it is also a sacrifice of self needs further developing.

The monk who is faithful to choir observance will find the Divine Office ascetically purifying as well as spiritually enlightening. In a hundred ways he will be learning control, learning humility, learning new facets to the mystery of charity.

There is the discipline of the senses: sight, voice, hearing have to

---

5 'Sing ye wisely.'—Ps. 46:7 quoted in Chapter 19 of the Holy Rule.

be subject to the mastery of the will. There is the discipline of the emotions: memory and imagination have to be silenced; curiosity, exasperation, enthusiasm, over-anxiety, over-sensitiveness at the confusion caused by our mistakes have to be curbed. There is the discipline of the reason and will: we shall think we know how better to conduct the choir, we shall want to assert ourselves in matters connected with pace and pitch and volume, we shall find ourselves the prey to doubts about the value of it all, to distractions, to desolations of spirit amounting to a positive suffering and even anguish, to temptations against each of our vows and to the religious state in general. The *Opus Dei* is a sacrifice.

But it is also a happiness. It is a happiness in the deepest sense, which includes such intangibles as an obscure sense of fitness, of worthwhileness, of belonging. It is the subtle satisfaction of understanding and being understood, of self-possession and being possessed by God.

In choir a monk comes to know, not only as a monk, but as a Christian and as a man, that he is verifying the purpose of his existence. There is satisfaction too in knowing that his own critical faculties, his own interests and appetites, are being denied so that the interests of others may be the better served.

The peace which the soul—not habitually, because that would lower its value, but from time to time—experiences in choir is different from the peace which is experienced in the cell. Solitude can give a peace to the soul which is unlike anything else in the world, but there is a peace of common purpose and common effort which can bring great strength. The Divine Office, crowning the life of charity in the community, can bring this peace.

So, it would be a mistake to look upon the choir simply as an arena where the soul is suffered to wrestle with beasts as at Ephesus. It would be a mistake to look upon it simply as a pulpit or platform for the work of the contemplative apostolate. A still greater mistake would be to look upon it as a stage for the performance of spectacles intended to edify. Substantially it is none of these things: substantially it is the meeting place where men dedicated to the service of God come together to proclaim, with minds and voices united, the majesty and goodness of God.

As in his private prayer, so in his public prayer, the choir-religious is a searcher. '*Quaerentes enim invenient Eum*', says St Augustine in his Confessions, '*et invenientes laudabunt Eum.*'[6] The psalms bear witness as much to his discovery as to his search. Truth, wisdom, beauty, love: all are imparted to the searching soul. And the soul's response to God is acknowledged: '*Sacrificium laudis honorificabit Me.*'[7]

Liturgical prayer, then, is designed to bring about the closest union of the soul with God. It is the ascent of charity within the mystical body *in odorem suavitatis*.[8] It is God's chosen form of prayer for man.

In the soul that worships by means of the liturgy there is no conflict of charity—the charity of action going one way and the charity of contemplation going another—for the whole being is surrendered to undivided love. The terms 'active' and 'contemplative' will, to such a soul, have only an academic value. The soul knows that if God wants the 'active' side of charity served, He will do so by applying to it the fruits of the 'contemplative'.

The love of Christ and the love of the members of His body are 'like two young roes that are twins which feed among the lilies'. The simile taken from the Canticle can be as suitably applied to prayer as to charity: prayer in choir and prayer in private are as twins nourished by the sacramental life of the Church and growing in the likeness of the perfect prayer of Christ.

---

6   Seeking indeed they shall find Him, and finding they shall praise Him.
7   'The sacrifice of praise shall honor Me.'—Ps. 49:24
8   In the odor of sweetness.

3

CONTEMPLATIVE PRAYER

IN the two foregoing chapters we have noted the interrelation between private and public prayer. In the present chapter we go on to examine the prayer to which this interrelation logically leads. The sequence is logical rather than actual, because there is no guarantee that the grace of contemplation will in fact follow the combined activities of mental and liturgical prayer.

It might be said, to make a loose précis of the definitions given by the authorities both patristic and modern, that contemplation is the calm loving exercise of intellect and will directed towards God and away from self and earthly things.

Man's goal on earth—even thinking of him as man, let alone as man of prayer—is to know God by faith and reason, to seek Him by hope and love, and to serve Him in truth. All this the contemplative— in his prayer humbly waiting upon God in loving confidence, and in work directing every energy and intention towards God—attempts to do.

In attempting to fulfil this purpose, the contemplative knows very well that at every moment he is dependent upon divine grace, and particularly upon the gifts of the Holy Ghost. He knows that there can be no Christian contemplation that has not the graces of baptism at its source or that mounts to God independently of His Church.

Viewed either from God's angle, from man's, or from the Church's angle, contemplation is the summit of the soul's endeavour. It is the way in which rational beings both fulfil their end on earth and already enjoy a share in God's eternal happiness.

To expand the traditional definitions of the contemplative act in operation, we can take Dionysius the Areopagite's description of the soul in contemplation 'leaving all things and entering within itself, gathering up its spiritual faculties and bringing them back into unity in such a manner that, enclosed as it were within a circle, its movements may no longer wander. Freed from external things, recollected within itself, returned to perfect simplicity … the movement of the soul is direct, when, instead of falling back upon itself it raises itself, by using external things as symbols, to a contemplation which is perfect in unity and purity.'

The first point to notice in the above passage is the idea of bringing the faculties back into unity, of the soul returning to simplicity. The implication is that from one cause or another the original order has been lost and must be restored by the combined work of grace and labour in contemplation.

Rational beings, whether angels or men, were created in the image and likeness of God. Man resembles God, as particularly the Greek fathers teach, under both heads: in image by reason and free will, in likeness by supernatural power. The affinity that exists between God and human souls is reaffirmed and developed in contemplation.

The other point in the quotation which particularly needs looking at is the statement that the soul, in its ascent to a contemplation which is perfect in unity and purity, 'uses external things as symbols'. Thus, Dionysius does not, as some would do, exclude liturgical prayer from contemplation.

In the early centuries of Christianity there was never any question of excluding the liturgy from even the highest stages of contemplation: psalmody was not to the fathers of the desert a prayer for beginners, or even a suitable occupation for contemplatives; it was an activity of contemplation, an exercise of the soul performed in unity and purity in virtue of its habit of contemplation.

It was not only an activity but *the* activity of the contemplative life.

Other activities, such as weaving mats and holding spiritual colloquies in common, took second place to the chanting of the psalter. A monk might meditate in his cell for long hours, but unless he had the psalms to act as both his quarry for prayer-material and his medium of prayer-expression he would not have been thought of as one who practised contemplation.

In later centuries, as man came to be, in religion as in art and thought, less theocentric and more anthropocentric, the idea of contemplation underwent a change: it lost some of its objective quality and concerned itself primarily with the strictly interior life.

Where contemplation is a purely personal affair, a matter exclusively for mental prayer, the life of the choir is obviously going to be looked upon by the contemplative as an unnecessary extra and even as a distraction. From about the late fourteenth century down to almost our own time this is more or less what the teachers of contemplation did think.

The tendency among modems is to go back to pre-renaissance spirituality, discounting the humanism which made man not only the focus-point of contemplative interest but also the co-efficient in almost equal partnership with the Holy Spirit, and to stress once more the objective element in contemplation.

Contemplation is love. Not the mechanism of love, but love. The first purpose of contemplation is not to know itself, to know how it works, to see how and where the dovetailing of grace and human efforts takes place. The contemplative waits upon God's love, waits upon the knowledge of God. Self-knowledge, like happiness and peace, is a by-product.

All we have to know about ourselves is our worthlessness. We know ourselves to be destined for good, and as objects of God's love possessed of a dignity which we know about but cannot realize, yet in our response to grace we are so ungenerous as to deserve nothing but scorn. '*Noverim me*', cries St Augustine, '*ut despiciam me*.'[1]

Contemplation exists to teach us other things besides our faults. It teaches us what we can never know by any other way. The light shed

---

[1] Would that I knew myself that I might despise myself.

by contemplation lights up not only what is in the soul, but also, and much more significantly, something of what is in God. The light of contemplation is a grace; it is not a clever examination of conscience or the natural power to concentrate on the thought of divine things.

The part played by the soul is that of disposing itself for the influx of grace. Contemplation is a gift that no personal human effort can lay claim to or merit. The soul can remove whatever is in the way of divine union, can open its eyes, can look in the right direction. God does the rest. But God is free to do or not to do—just as the soul is free to look away again or shut its eyes.

Thus, contemplation is a receiving act and not, essentially, a contributing act. The higher the soul mounts in the mystical life the more theopathic—acted upon by God, passive under the influence of divine grace—it becomes.

God may act on the soul directly or indirectly, now in one way and now in another. Some souls He initiates gradually, others in a moment. To some souls He imparts Himself by means of natural symbols, to others by means of the liturgy or solitude or the particular kind of interior prayer that is being practised. '*Verbum Dei non est alligatum*.'[2]

Mention must be made at this point of the distinction between acquired and infused contemplation. The terms came in as a result of the question which naturally suggests itself: can the soul acquire the habit of contemplation by being faithful to the ordinary graces, or does it have to be the recipient of grace which is special and mystical? An amplification of the terms should answer this.

Acquired contemplation (which is not really contemplation at all, but consideration aided by grace) is held to be present where there is a knowledge of God and creatures, where this knowledge is accompanied by love, where grace has guided the intellect and will to the possession of this loving knowledge, but where the resulting prayer is as much the fruit of industry as of grace.

In this kind of contemplation grace is at work because man is, and man is at work because grace is. Without one or the other there

---

2 The Word of God is not bound.

would be no prayer. The contemplation is 'acquired' by actively helping the Holy Ghost.

In his book *The Mystical Evolution*, Father Arintero compares such prayer to the simple, almost intuitive, act by which a theologian who has prepared his thesis prayerfully can view the subject without reasoning.

Contemplation which is infused is something quite different. Here the main work is done by the Holy Spirit, and the soul concurs. The act of contemplation is now the result, not of having understood the subject so thoroughly as to see it in a single act without need of reasoning, but of divine inspiration.

The inspiration may come to the soul through one of various different channels, even through a badly written book or a badly prepared sermon, but the point is that it leads the soul to contemplate God lovingly and simply and without the deliberation that was required in the case of 'acquired' contemplation. All the soul has to do in this exercise is to consent.

'Infused or passive contemplation', says St Thomas, 'is in us without our deliberating it, though not without our consenting to it.' It is therefore not a prayer which we can make when we want to: we can never be certain that the divine inspiration will answer to the movement of our will.

Another reason why this kind of prayer is called 'infused' contemplation is that, more directly than in the case of acquired contemplation, it is the prayer-expression of the infused virtues.

Merely in passing it might be noted that neither St John of the Cross nor St Teresa recognizes 'acquired' contemplation: for them the label would be simply 'discursive prayer'. For these authorities the term 'contemplation' would denote passive prayer.

St Benedict does not mention the word 'contemplation' at all, whether acquired or infused. But since his whole purpose is to train souls towards union with God, the omission of the word is immaterial. The Holy Rule is contemplative in character, the daily life is orientated towards contemplation, elements which hinder contemplation are removed.

When St Thomas says, 'it is necessary that by burning charity our wills be turned towards God: this is to have a heart made ready for divine union', it is not necessary for him to speak specifically of contemplation: he can leave off there and we grasp what he is leading up to. When St Benedict speaks about the Divine Office, about silence and enclosure and the love of Christ, he can leave off there and we grasp what he is leading up to.

Action, in the mind of St Benedict, is a sideline; the main activity in the monastery is the abiding acknowledgment of God's presence. The monastery is a school of God's service, a training-ground for men of faith. As a material of psychological necessity, action may have to be taken up for a time as in the case of helping with the harvest—but it is not an essential part of the life. The arts may be given their measure of attention, and the crafts will come in useful for the support of the community, but these are not the things that the community stands for. The community stands for the life of prayer.

A measured activity is inevitable and desirable in a monastery: the service of God would be lifeless without it. But it must be controlled or it will get out of hand and stifle the interior life of the community. The spirit of the house must be predominantly the spirit that begets humility, simplicity, recollection; not the spirit that begets large-scale enterprise and publicity.

'But what', it may be objected, 'about the care of souls? Have monks the right to hide themselves away when there are souls to be saved by apostolic work?' Though the point has been touched upon in the chapter on liturgical prayer, it is one which needs confirmation in relation to the contemplative life as a mode of existence.

The life of a contemplative monastery is its own apostolate. The principle is clearly and authoritatively stated by Pope Pius XI in his *Umbralitatem* addressed to the Carthusian Order: 'Christian society has received great services from the monastic institution, the sole aim of which is the exclusive dedication of the monks to contemplation of heavenly realities, each one living in the secrecy of his cell, free and exempt from any external ministry.'

The external ministry is carried on by men whose vocation it is to be external ministers. God has called them to it. 'Those who have embraced the life of seclusion', states the same Apostolic Constitution, 'in order to contemplate the divine mysteries and eternal truths, to offer ceaseless supplication for the expansion of His kingdom and to atone for their own sins, and above all for those of their brethren through voluntary mortifications of mind and body as prescribed by the Rule, we are entitled to state that they have undoubtedly chosen the best part as Mary of Bethany did. If the Lord calls to it, there is no condition or way of life more perfect to be proposed to the choice and holy ambition of men.'

On this showing a Benedictine monastery that does its essential work within its enclosure, keeping up the liturgical life and remaining faithful to the Holy Rule, needs no active work for souls to justify its existence. It is its own justification. Its hidden life is its work for souls. The old idea—as found in Cassian, for instance, and therefore in monasticism generally until the beginning of the decline in the Middle Ages—was that monastic 'activity' was conditioned not so much by the needs of the world outside as by the needs of the monks inside. One reason for this is that the needs of the world were not so pressing then as they are now, and that there were bishops and priests to attend to them.

On economic and psychological grounds an active work could be looked upon as a good thing for monks. But only under certain conditions, only if the ideal of keeping the monastery as a self-contained unit was being found to create worse problems than it solved.

Activity according to St Thomas is *per se* a hindrance to contemplation. The act of contemplating and the act of caring for souls cannot be performed at the same time. But activity, he adds, may *per accidens* foster contemplation in an individual soul and further the contemplative life in a community.

If the above principle is misunderstood, it gives to monks and monasteries a liberty which is exceedingly dangerous. The doctrine, found also but less explicitly in St Gregory who belongs to the next generation after St Benedict, means that where there is question of exercising certain virtues and subduing certain vices—in other words, where there is need for an outlet without which the harmony of the contemplative life would be disturbed—activity can be said to further contemplation.

It sounds like a quibble, but in fact is not one. The history of monasticism and of individual religious houses shows that sometimes the contemplative character of the life can be preserved only by the admission of certain well-regulated active works. But they have to be very well-regulated, or they will, as already suggested, encroach more and more.

Having treated of the nature of contemplation and the policy to be pursued in safeguarding it, we have come now to consider what the soul does in prayer to dispose towards it.

The prayer of the contemplative soul—the soul that is disposing itself for grace, whether the grace that God sends shall turn out to be the grace of infused contemplation or the ordinary graces necessary to continue in ordinary prayer—is roughly the acknowledgment which St Peter made at the Transfiguration.

'Lord, it is good for us to be here.'[3] We do not know what awaits us; we do not ask. We do not look back at the past; we trust that our sins have been forgiven. We do not use this light of grace in order to examine ourselves; we use it so that it may show us more of You. In the meantime, we are in the right place.

It is 'good for us' not only in the sense that we like being here, but also in the sense that it is the best place for us to be: here we can adore You in spirit and in truth. We do not adore You enough, even here, but placed as we are we know that You are indeed worthy of all adoration, and this is what we want to give You.

'Looking up, they saw only Jesus.'[4]

This disposition of soul may or may not lead to infused contemplation; certainly, it is the right disposition for it. To 'see only Jesus' is not necessarily, even in the most advanced stages of contemplation, to be constantly aware of the Sacred Humanity. Even in the specific act of contemplation, as distinct from the habit of contemplation, the nearness of Christ may be unfelt.

The vision fades, and, like the disciples, the soul comes down from Tabor. Like the disciples, the soul is ready to yield to the new form

---

3 Matthew 17:4
4 Matthew 17:8

which His presence takes. 'If I go not, the Paraclete will not come to you... it is expedient for you that I go.'[5] It is the same with Mary at the tomb: I am not yet ascended to My Father ... do not cling to your former knowledge of Me but adapt yourself to the new form that I shall take.

Adaptation to the spirit, replacement of the natural by the supernatural, forgetting the material and stretching out to the eternal and infinite, the soul comes to a way of apprehending which is of faith and not of feeling.

The fruit of this faith is unreflecting trust. 'Whatever You say, Lord ... whatever You want.' It is simple, outgoing, calm. We see it in the attitude of Mary of Bethany seated before Christ, unanxious about any other responsibility—even that of helping her sister.

We see it in St Paul who, whether present or absent, was always with the Lord. For Christ to dwell in our hearts, for Christ to be formed in us and for us to be formed in Christ, we must put off the shell of our former lives and come out into the light of grace. 'Blessed are the clean of heart, for they shall see God.'[6] The heart and mind and will are cleansed in the nights of sense and spirit written about by St John of the Cross. Now, and now only, can the light of infused contemplation shine through.

The process so far traced, then, is this: the soul is drawn along the way towards contemplation in the course of its ordinary prayer; it is brought to an increasing knowledge of God by means of the gifts of the Holy Spirit; it uses this knowledge to foster love; love, taking new inspiration under the influx of love itself, comes to rest in the object of its desire.

Always the soul must remember that love, not knowledge, is the goal of its desire. It comes to the same thing in the end, but in the business of searching it is easier to get slowed down in the outskirts of knowledge than in the outskirts of love.

St Thomas says that whereas the knowledge of human things is better than the love of them, the love of divine things is better than the knowledge of them. But whether at the summit of contemplation

---

5   John 16:7
6   Matthew 5:8

it is the intellect or the will that is principally engaged we need not here concern ourselves. It is contemplation in religious life rather than in speculative theology that calls for attention in the present chapter.

As the act is, so is the habit which rises out of the act. As the habit is, so is the act which the habit engenders.

In habit and act, contemplation brings peace: the soul rests in the bare fact of God. Not in the proximity, but in the reality. The soul knows, without having to experience the comfort of it, that 'the Lord is close to those that call upon Him, to those who call upon Him in truth.'[7]

We have treated of peace at some length when stressing the need for order and control. But when all is said, peace is nothing else than God present in the soul. When the soul knows that God is present, there is no need to taste the sweets of peace, or the sweets of God's presence. The knowledge is enough.

Long after the soul has resigned itself to the deprivation of every other feeling it will still go on wanting the feeling of peace. Peace comes only when the soul does not want it first.

Every now and then peace will flood the soul of the contemplative, as it does with everyone, but the peace which comes of contemplation is different from this. There is one peace that is enjoyed in the sensitive nature, and another that is possessed in the depths of the soul itself.

Peace can be so deeply anchored in the will that it is hardly noticed on the surface. And because it is substantial and not superficial it is not valued: the soul would prefer a peace which can be enjoyed and wallowed in.

To the objection that a peace which is so deep that it cannot be perceived is no peace at all, it must be answered that such a peace can be perceived but not by the senses. The faculty which recognizes such a peace is the intellect enlightened by faith. But there are many souls who do not like having to use this faculty any more than they have to. Faith is not a comfortable light to see by. So true peace is very often missed.

---

7   Psalm 144:18

The life of contemplation is the life of faith. When the soul has learned in contemplation that God is all, there follows a comprehensive serenity which is proof against the enemies of peace.

In drawing the soul closer to truth itself, contemplation brings the soul to another and a higher level of perception. Faith, not sense, does the apprehending. Faith is now the eye of the soul. Faith gives a new meaning to ideas as well as to facts. The old idea of peace gives place to the new.

The old idea of light, of happiness, of reality, and even of love is seen to cover less than half the reality as it is in the sight of God. The light which is life, the *lumen vitae*, transforms the world. It is this by which the contemplative lives and by which he learns new aspects of the will of God: it is the light of love and faith.

Such, then, is contemplation, habit and act: waiting in stillness, trust, love. Not waiting for mystical experiences or mystical knowledge, but for whatever God wants—for whatever will enable the soul to love more. 'Behold the handmaid of the Lord; be it done according to thy word.'[8]

Thus, those who claim that contemplative and liturgical prayer are mutually exclusive are misunderstanding either one or the other; perhaps both. If one of the accepted texts of contemplation, taken from the Canticle, gives a picture of the bride's dual activity—'I sleep and my heart watcheth'—then surely the same dual activity can be allowed to the contemplative praying in choir. 'I sing and my heart watcheth,' the soul can say, 'I rise up and open to my beloved ... I have found Him whom my soul loveth, and I have brought Him into my house.'[9]

But it is by faith and not by touch that we find Him—by a contemplation which gives assurance rather than awareness, conviction rather than any formulated consciousness of His Being. Though the discovery may teach us little that we can sort out and store away for reference, it certainly teaches humility and brings strength. Even if it reveals nothing more at the time but the immediacy of God's will, it

---

8 Luke 1:38
9 Canticle of Canticles 5:2, 3:4

has fulfilled a primary purpose. But as the grace is responded to the horizon widens, till eventually it is filled by God.

4

RECOLLECTION

LITURGICAL and contemplative prayer find their corresponding activity—indeed are continued—in heaven. Recollection is for this world only.

Recollection is the act of gathering the faculties of the soul and holding them at the pleasure of God. In heaven we shall be forever in the presence of God; on earth we have to put ourselves in it.

The best way to put ourselves in the presence of God is to acknowledge the presence of God in us. The indwelling is a fact of theology, not a flight of the mind.

By faith we recognize God as present; by love we unite ourselves with Him and with His will. Faith and love: not imagination and feeling.

But though in heaven we shall not have to recollect ourselves as we do on earth when we want to advert to His presence, we shall exercise the same faculties—namely, the intellect and will.

Recollection, in its original and strictest sense, is neither love nor prayer: it is the summoning of scattered powers. But it has come to mean more than preparation: it means loving possession.

Recollection is not the same as the set act of mental prayer, which is taken to be an exercise apart, but is rather an attention to God present in the soul. As such it may be the result of industry aided by grace, and accordingly part of 'applied' or 'acquired' contemplation, or it may be one of the fruits of infused contemplation and accordingly a special grace from God.

Whether the grace of God's presence is ordinary or extraordinary, the prayer of recollection covers a great range. It can be applied to the first movements of the soul towards God before any sort of articulation has properly begun, and it can be applied to the habit engendered in the soul by passive unions.

The recollection of our Lady gives us the clearest light on this prayer: 'Mary kept all these words, pondering them in her heart.' Her recollection was at once retrospective, actual, and preparatory.

Recollection therefore is an anticipation of mental prayer, an act continued and intensified during mental prayer, and an extension and expansion of mental prayer when the time allotted to it is over.

Taken in such a sense, the recollection of a soul is the soul's interior life. It is the climate which brings out the gifts and which conduces directly to union. It is the response to grace and the life of faith, hope, and love. It is not surprising therefore that St Benedict gives it a great deal of attention. A monastery without it would be an odd sort of monastery.

Recollection for St Benedict is not just a devout practice to be urged upon novices in the hope that some will feel sufficiently attracted to it as to keep it up in later life. It is not a devotion; it is a habit of mind which a man must acquire if he is to serve God with any degree of perfection.

'The foundation of the interior life according to St Benedict', says Father Merton, 'is the presence of God. St Benedict wants to write a rule that will make it impossible for those who really follow its spirit to deal with God as an abstraction, a hidden and anonymous power. This is one of the most essential features of the Rule to which all exterior observances are obviously ordered.' What is said here of a particular rule and a particular founder will be taken to apply generally. All religious, whether or not it is formulated for them in as many words, will need to base their spirituality on knowledge *per praesentiam*.

In the mystical state this knowledge of God's presence is an experience in the strict sense: an experience of the supernatural operation of God in the soul. The soul, as Father Merton points out, knows God in contemplation by an act of *His* love which gives experimental certitude. It is not the soul's love first, but God's. Knowing that it is loved by Him as Father, Friend, and Spouse, and that He works interiorly towards union with Him, the soul appreciates—'*per effectum amoris filialis*,'[1] says St Thomas—the extent to which its own love is dependent upon God's.

But what about the non-mystical state? St Benedict insists that he is writing for beginners in the spiritual life, so clearly does not envisage such an experience of the special divine action in the ordinary run of his monks. Only a percentage in a community will be contemplatives, *pati divina*, and it is the saint's object to mould those who are not contemplatives as well as those who are. Even the most naturally active can be trained in the practice of the presence of God.

'Let him remember that he is always seen by God ... that his actions lie open to the eye of God ... we believe that the divine presence is everywhere ... let him say with the prophet *I have been brought to nothing and I knew it not; I am become as a beast before thee and am always with thee.*' St Benedict, addressing neophytes but forming contemplatives, shows the way to the closest union with God.

Constant acknowledgment of God's presence leads to two things: care in the performance of every act, however insignificant in itself, and a recognition of the divine indwelling which leads ultimately to mystical union.

The soul that is habituated to the presence of God is habituated to the will of God. If recollection makes actual the presence of God to the soul, it makes actual in the same way God's will.

The will of God, like the presence of God, may seem at first to be something which the soul has to look for outside itself. But as the soul continues in its search it comes to know that the will and the presence of God are both closer home. 'It is by His will, which obedience makes our own will,' says Father Merton, 'that God enters into us intimately as our friend. This union of wills is what leads to our identification with our Beloved.'

In St Benedict's conception of spirituality, based as we have seen

---

[1] Through the effect of filial love.

upon the presence of God and man's knowledge of his utter worthlessness, the soul mounts from fear to love: from fear of God's ever-watching eye to love of His indwelling presence and will.

Beginning with obedience to a divine authority which is present but outside itself, the soul moves on to concurrence with that same authority manifesting itself within

St Benedict does not bother himself about distinctions between ordinary and extraordinary grace, between the purgative and the illuminative and unitive way, between active and passive prayer. He pins his faith to 'the beholding of God in every place'.

Where the will of God is taken to be the only thing that matters, the textbook stages of the spiritual life are unimportant. The stage you are in is the will of God, and you give Him the greatest glory you can from there.

Where there is identification with Christ, the idea of superior or inferior ways of prayer is meaningless.

United with the infinite and eternal good, the idea of first, second, and third has no value. God is all, and the time sequence of temporal spirituality is swallowed up in that.

When the soul is in the presence of God, and when the presence of God is in the soul, there is neither Jew nor Greek: God's love and will are everywhere. There is no right and left in heaven.

The development of the practice of the presence of God, as in the case of the development of humility, is the work of grace. 'All this our Lord will bring about by the Holy Spirit in His servant,' says St Benedict concluding his seventh chapter, 'now that he is cleansed from defects and sins.'

Thus, recollection becomes a drawing into itself on the soul's part not so much by force or by fear as by the gravitational attraction of the Holy Spirit's presence within. The indwelling is the magnet, and the soul yields to the pull of grace.

The magnetism is exercised through love: not the soul's love, but God's. 'I have loved thee with an everlasting love,' says the Lord in the prophecy of Jeremias, 'therefore I have drawn thee.'[2]

What God crowns in the soul is not the soul's goodness, but His

---

[2] Jeremiah 31:3

own; not the soul's beauty or perfection or merit, but His own. The soul is made in the image of God, and it is the likeness that gives Him glory.

The more fully the soul yields to the presence of God within itself, the more 'like' does it become. The closer the resemblance, the deeper the appreciation of Him who is resembled. The deeper also the understanding of that self which is taking on a new likeness.

Habitually trying to live interiorly with God, the soul comes upon the doctrine of the Incarnation both more comprehensively and more immediately. It sees how Christ, in taking the nature of man, identified Himself not only with all humanity but with every member of it. The infinite act of God is pinpointed upon me: I am loved personally by Christ: He is here, in me, now.

If the source of all is present in my soul at this moment, if He who is the beginning and the end resides in me and I in Him, I must be enjoying a foretaste of eternity. He who is 'yesterday and today and the same forever' has given me a share in His eternal life. Where I am now, and as I stand, *I possess God*.

The strange thing is that this fact may be written down and read, yet may mean very little. The words may lie dead upon the page. The implication is that for the deeper understanding of a truth we need to live with it. To give a notional assent is one thing—and it is a good thing, requiring the act of faith—but it is quite another to experience the reality of what is assented to.

To live with this particular truth is to be recollected. Even to give a notional assent, and to repeat the act till it becomes second nature to do so, is to be recollected. It means then that the assent is notional no longer, but actual and habitual.

But whatever the way that has led to it, the establishment of the presence of God as the primary practice of the spiritual life is highly significant: the soul is now consciously in its proper element.

The word 'consciously' may here be misleading. The significant stage is reached when the soul is conscious, from its experience of the inward operation of grace, of the importance of recollecting itself constantly and living as much as possible in the presence of God. The consciousness need not extend to the form which the presence of God takes.

A soul, as suggested in the foregoing chapter, may be very little aware of the companionship of Christ. In fact, the more the soul advances into the cloud of contemplation the less sensible will the companionship become. The soul will not feel, nor see, nor imagine Christ. Instead, in an obscure and in a quite undevotional way, it will know Him as present.

We may be talking to a man when the lights go out. We are left in the dark, and the conversation trails off into silence. For the whole night there may be no further word spoken, no sound to suggest the presence of the other person. We forget about him and follow our own thoughts. We do not know what part of the room he is in. We do not picture him; we need not be wondering about him at all. We may even go to sleep and wake up and trace the course of our dreams. But all the time at the back of our mind we know that he is there. If he were to say a word, we would not have to wonder who had spoken. If someone else were to mention him, we would relate at once what was said. 'He is here all the time', we would say, 'in the dark.'

A soul coming from a discursive and imaginative knowledge of God's presence to this contemplative knowledge which is of faith may find itself disappointed at the dryness of it. Such a soul will feel cheated, will feel tempted to value the sensible presence more. It will feel like a child arriving at a party only to find that there is no cream in the meringues: it will wish it had stayed at home where at least one had custard to put in the meringues.

But if such a soul experiments in trying to recapture its earlier experience of the presence of God, it will not advance in the way of faith. To cling to a presentation of Christ because it is the familiar presentation is not to cling to Christ.

In the work of dwelling habitually with God in the spirit we may not dwell in a memory. The material which made for the memory must go now to the making of faith. Divine love dwells, not in observation or tender retrospection, but in surrender and trust.

Though the presence of God enjoyed contemplatively in the soul is often apprehended without devotion, it is never apprehended without strength. What the contemplative soul misses in the way of consolation is more than made up for in the way of an increased faith.

Possessing Truth Itself and Absolute Being, the soul depends less and less upon the support of creatures. The craving for human sympathy dwindles in proportion as the understanding of the divine nature grows. Selfish preoccupations fade into insignificance before the one reality which is God.

Though in theory it should not be difficult to remain recollected with Him in whom 'we live and move and have our being', it does in fact demand, besides faith, considerable effort and vigilance.

'We must build up this edifice of all the virtues', says Cassian, 'and preserve our minds from all manner of distraction so that they may become gradually accustomed to the contemplation of God.' And again in the colloquy following: 'The more the soul withdraws from the sight of material things, the more is it purified and enabled to see Jesus Christ, either in the humiliations of His life or in the majesty of His glory ... they contemplate His divinity with a pure eye who turn away from earthly thoughts and works to mount with Him the high peak of solitude, where they contemplate by the light of their faith the beauty of His face.'

Cassian's is only another way of saying 'blessed are the clean of heart for they shall see God', but note how he says that we must cleanse our hearts if contemplation is to cleanse our vision for us. And that, even then, we see by the light of faith and not effort of sense.

If purity of heart were either a matter of natural habit or of grace automatically bestowed, it would not be a beatitude.

So, the man who aspires to union with God in prayer must set himself to live above the tumult. He must not only shed as far as possible useless cares and interests but also contrive to keep serene among cares and interests which are not useless and which are his responsibility.

'And touch not the wall, that the bride may sleep in greater security.' There must be a wall of peace, says St John of the Cross commenting on this line in the Canticle, to act as defence against the disturbances which threaten 'the garden enclosed'. The bride must be at rest, untroubled both by distractions from without and by anxieties within, if she is to know the love that the Bridegroom has for her.

5
THE MEANS

RELIGIOUS tradition provides a variety of ways by which recollection may be preserved; personal experience provides others. Though devout customs, whether learned from others or of one's own making, do not guarantee recollection—because nothing can guarantee a grace—they can at least be made to promote it.

Broadly speaking, it might be said that recollection is fostered mainly by curbing one's natural impetuosity, by avoiding disagreement and controversy, and by a careful planning and use of one's time. But it is the factors more immediately relating to recollection that will be discussed in this chapter and the next. The remote means are either contained or assumed in the principles laid down for the direction of the religious life; the proximate means need enumeration.

One advantage which recollection has over both liturgical and set mental prayer is that it does not have to be interrupted. The whole idea is that it should be spun out over the day. While working at a desk or in a field, while on a journey or in a hospital, a man can make a choir and sanctuary within the cell of his own soul.

But though independent, physically, of breviary and prie-dieu, recollection is not independent of all outside help: prayer material has to be collected, stored, supplied to the intellect and will when wanted.

At some times the soul will be more conscious of this need than at others. In the advanced stages of mystical union all its reserves are within.

> My soul is occupied,
> And all my substance is in His service;
> Now I guard no flock,
> Nor have I any other employment:
> My sole occupation is love.

But until this stage is reached (given in the twenty-eighth stanza by St John of the Cross), the soul must 'of emeralds and of flowers in the early morning gathered, make garlands flowering in Thy love'. Only then, when the soul has 'entered into the heart of the thicket' and has reached 'the deep caverns of the rock which are all secret', is there no longer any need of outward help.

Chief among the direct means towards deepening the life of prayer—silence and solitude being thought of as elements or safeguards of prayer rather than as providing material for it—is what St Benedict calls *lectio divina*. The term is taken to mean more than the daily half-hour of spiritual reading to which most religious are bound by the regulations of their order.

Lectio divina can be translated as the meditative study of divine things. It covers the prayerful reading of Holy Scripture, the works of the Fathers and mystics, devotional and liturgical literature. It supposes that a considerable time each day is spent in its exercise. In the monasteries under St Benedict this 'holy reading' occupied between three and four hours a day almost the whole year round; only for a short period at midsummer was it reduced to less.

Obedience may send a monk to study secular subjects, but his spiritual leaning should be towards *lectio divina*. His particular ability may involve him in accountancy, his creative talent may send him to the arts, his work

for the community may make him virtually a mechanic or chemist or cook, but all the time he should know that the study appropriate to his state is the study of divine things.

Though a monk must find sanctity in doing the work that is given him by authority, he should still hanker after the work that is given him by the spirit of his rule. When not obliged by his secular employments to works which are only indirectly related to God, he must find his way back to the more direct service of God in recollection. He must accustom himself to the renewal of *lectio divina*.

The richest quarry of prayer-material is obviously revelation itself: nothing can teach us more about the presence of God than the inspiration of God. '*Disce cor Dei*', says St Gregory, '*in verbis Dei*.'[1] To be ignorant of Scripture is to be ignorant, according to St Jerome, of Christ.

The arrested spiritual progress of certain souls may well be accounted for by their lack of interest in the Scriptures. Not having bothered to study the Old and New Testaments they suffer the same blindness, and culpably so in their case, as that of the Ethiopian under Candace to whom Philip the deacon explained the prophecy of Isaias in the desert. 'Of whom does the prophet speak? Of himself or of some other man?'[2]

Or perhaps such souls have studied, but studied in the wrong way. If we study academically, we can hardly hope to profit spiritually. We must hunger and thirst after the justice of God, not only after the knowledge of the text. After thirty or forty years in religion it will be painful to hear the reproach, 'So long a time have I been with you, and you have not known Me.'[3]

There must be order and spirit and discipline in scriptural study. Study, even of divine things, must be kept in its place: it is a means, not an end. To make the Scriptures take the place of prayer is to see in false perspective.

'But at least when I study the Bible I am thinking about God,' the soul may say, 'whereas when I go to prayer I think about nothing.' Prayer, nevertheless, is the more important exercise of the two. The will may not be starved in order to feed the intellect.

To study the Scriptures without further reference to prayer would

---

1 Learn the heart of God in the words of God.
2 Acts 8:34
3 John 14:9

be like making all the preparations for the holocaust and then leaving it unlit.

'Gedeon went in and boiled a kid and made unleavened loaves of a measure of flour, and putting the flesh in a basket, and the broth of the flesh in a pot, he carried all under the oak, and presented it to the angel. And the angel of the Lord said to him: Take the flesh and the unleavened loaves, and lay them upon that rock and pour out the broth thereon. And when he had done so, the angel of the Lord put forth the tip of the rod which he held in his hand and touched the flesh and the unleavened loaves, and there arose a fire from the rock and consumed the flesh and the unleavened loaves; and the angel of the Lord vanished out of his sight.'[4]

Much goes into the arranging of sacrifice, but more goes into its consummation. The difference is that where man makes ready, God makes absolute. The fruit of man's study—a mixed oblation placed on a hard rock—goes up in a flame of worship before the Lord. It is not for man to decide the moment when the tip of the angel's rod shall touch the result of his labour, but when that moment comes he will know that he has not laboured in vain.

What has been said of the study of the Scriptures may be taken to apply equally to the study of the Fathers. But when we come to treat of theological study, we are not treading quite the same ground: we have to leave Cassian and St Benedict for Cassiodorus. But even Cassiodorus, whose approach to monastic studies was the scholar's rather than the mystic's, has to be left behind if we consider the evolution of monasticism's intellectual life under the influence of the schoolmen of the Middle Ages.

Once learning and culture are introduced into monastic life you have to make special provision to guard against the swamping of the purely spiritual side: scholarship for the sake of scholarship is as much a distraction as food for the sake of food.

Thus, because it is harder for most people to turn their theology than their Scripture into a prayer, it is all the more necessary to stress

---

[4] Judges 6:19-21

the prayer-content of theological study. Theology, no less than God's revealed word, points towards union with God. Its very name teaches us this.

A man may view theology in one of three ways. He may think of it as he would think of a fire-extinguisher—something which he had better know something about but which he does not want to have occasion to use. He may think of it as he would a slot-machine—something which will provide him with an answer to his need even though it may not be the brand he is accustomed to. He may think of it, lastly, as he would think of electricity—that is, hardly thinking of it consciously at all, but going to it every day and night for his cooking, his heating, his lighting, his laundry and even for much of his listening and looking.

The man of prayer is living against a background of theology. It should become as natural to him to think theologically as to speak correctly or to breathe evenly.

To think theologically is not the same as to think technically. A man may know little of the jargon of theology but much of its significance.

The man who scorns theology on the grounds that he will not be examined on his text-book knowledge but on his gospel charity is mistaking the whole function of theology. Theology ministers to charity. That is the whole point of it.

In a sense theology is charity: the science of God and the science of love are not two sciences but one. *Deus caritas est.*

The more the soul knows of God, consequently, the more it knows of love. Theology exists in order to explain to us the source of love. Like Scripture, it reveals the nature and the mind of God. Like Scripture, it expresses God's will, and lays down the terms of God's will.

The man who thinks he can be religious and spiritual without knowing why he must be religious and spiritual is like a man who thinks he can be faithful to a wife without knowing why a wife should deserve it of him. He will not be able to maintain it.

Theology, then, is not primarily a thing of the brain but of the soul. It is the soul that grows by means of theology. The capacity to know the truths of theology grows too, and this in turn helps the soul.

Of the gifts of the Holy Ghost, that of wisdom is accounted the highest. Theology may not be wisdom, but it gives the knowledge that leads to it.

Without some degree of wisdom born of theology, how shall a man help others in their difficulties of faith? It is not only those whose vocation it is to teach, preach, and hear confessions who are asked questions about God.

Without reason to fall back upon, how shall a man maintain his own life of faith when his feelings have spent themselves? Where there is no theology behind him, he will look for the sensation of faith elsewhere; he will experiment in false religion.

The intellect is not the whole man, but neither is the heart the whole man. If the heart misses a beat, the head can still survive; if the head aches, the heart goes on as usual. But though reason may not be everything, the presumption is that if there is nothing of reason in the head there is very little of will in the heart.

If there is only sentiment in the heart, the life of the soul will not be the life of faith and love but of mood. The will cannot be expected to bear the twofold burden of an unreasoning intellect and a sentimental heart.

The will makes itself responsible for its work only when the mind and heart are ready to co-operate. Neither mind, heart, nor will can manage on its own. Of the three it is heart, by which here is meant the emotions, that is the least reliable.

Though theology exists chiefly to train the mind in the things of God, it exists also to train the will and the emotions. In the science of God nothing may be left out on the part of man.

Though theology's work is chiefly in the cause of faith, its work is also in the cause of love and the conduct of love. A man must be able to think before he is able to love.

Theology does not exist to save man the trouble of searching; it exists to save man the agony of doubting. Man will always have to search, and it may be his temptation to doubt, but if he has a right understanding of theology his search will be forwarded and his doubt arrested.

Besides leading to faith and wisdom, a right understanding of theology leads the soul to humility, obedience, unity and simplicity of spirit, wonder at the majesty of God, and so to recollection and worship; a wrong understanding of theology leads the soul to puffed up vanity, guesswork, multiplicity, and distraction. Vain speculation and the knowledge that inflates: this is what a wrong understanding means.

But why all this talk about the difference between knowledge and love, intellect and will? They ought to speak of the same thing. It is we with our piecemeal, departmental, empirical minds that make these separations. God dwells in unity, and the nearer the soul approaches God the more unified should its life become.

'For the union of two, the extremities of each must correspond.' If the soul is to be united with God, it must have learned to draw into one the diversity of its operations. Not only must the study of Scripture and the study of theology assist one another and achieve a harmony, but the knowledge resulting from their combined activity must lead on to prayer. Recollection is not a dream: it is the effect brought about by grace under the immediate instrumentality of causes lying within the control of man.

Another of these factors which directly forward the habit of recollection is, if it is allowed to and if it is done properly, manual labour.

St Benedict saw in manual labour a variety of advantages, all of them vital to a religious community: it killed idleness, provided for the needs of the monastery, disciplined the body, expressed obedience. In his own monasteries he regulated for at least five and a half hours a day of manual work. From the middle of May till the middle of August the time amounted to nine hours.[5]

That so large a proportion of the monk's day should be given to labour—which besides agriculture might mean cutting down trees, hedging and ditching, building, making roads, work in the dairy stables, green-house, bakehouse, mill—is not so surprising when we realize that the whole of St Benedict's monasticism rests on the balance of three things: prayer, *lectio*, manual labour.

---

5 The monk's horarium in St Benedict's time, differing according to the seasons, is given by Abbot Butler in his *Benedictine Monachism*, pp. 280-288.

The triangle of Benedictine works—the work of God in the choir, the work of the mind and will in the cell, the work of the body in physical toil—must be kept even. It is not a question of hours apportioned but of interest given. If undue stress is laid upon one aspect of the life, the other two are weakened.

This is not the place to discuss anything so controversial as the kind of work most suited to the monk, whether to the monk of early or later monasticism, but so far as the mind of St Benedict is concerned the subject is not open to question.

Though it may be exceptional in any given monastery for monks to do manual labour in their free time, it should not be extraordinary. To follow a course which goes back to St Benedict himself, and for which special legislation is made in the Holy Rule, can hardly be to lay oneself open to the charge of singularity.

Given the approval of the abbot, the regular practice of manual labour cannot but be of service to the monk's soul. It is a discipline, an outlet, an education, and, if the monk has his wits about him, a prayer.

Taken simply as an *ascesis*, a hard thing done in the spirit of sacrifice, it has value. It has far more value taken positively as an expression of service. Submission, body and mind, to the supernatural order as found in the natural order, is active homage.

If manual labour is not an expression of the monk's service it may well be an expression of the monk's self. The test will lie in how he responds to the sanctions attaching to manual labour.

If I go out when there is fruit to be picked but stay in when there is tar to be spread, I am treating manual labour as a pastime. Toil is going to help my soul only if I make no distinctions. If the choice of work is left to me, the qualification should not be comfort or personal taste but recollection.

Always the criterion is recollection. Digging is more conducive to prayer than mending a roof; but if I happen to be a person who can find God more easily on a housetop than in a field, I may freely opt for manual labour on the roof.

Manual labour is to prayer what carpentry is to carving, what masonry is to sculpture. There are sculptors who insist that those who want to learn from them should first serve an apprenticeship as labourers in a stone quarry: this will give them the feel of the medium. The connection between manual labour and prayer can be even closer than this.

If, again, I do manual labour only when the weather is fine, I am clearly not serious in my approach to it. One of the conditions should be that I work in all weathers and when I do not feel like working. Not until my body has got worn into the variations of the climate can I really benefit by what creation has to teach me about the natural and the supernatural.

Habitual and solitary work in the open, work which looks for no more interest than what the rhythm of the seasons can supply, is not only purifying and humbling but strangely enlightening.

The soul finds itself acquiring a less temporal view of life and of the universe. The world, its beauty and its history, is seen in truer perspective; more comprehensively. New standards seem to be learned for the measurement of time. Space too, under the sky, yields some of its secrets.

In such a way do eternity and infinity seem closer to the man who works on the soil than they do to the man who works on a machine or at a desk. Perhaps it is that contact with the elemental things brings a kind of elemental wisdom which civilization tends to overlay.

From science, history, philosophy man learns truth; but at several removes. Nor does he learn the whole truth directly from nature—because if he did there would be no need for revelation or for a Church— but he does learn something about God's creation which only an experimental knowledge can give. The first thing that this understanding teaches him is his littleness.

'Remember, man, that thou art dust, and unto dust thou shalt return.'[6] You might think that the act of breaking the earth, driving furrows through it, draining it, sowing and reaping it would give to man a sense of mastery. The soil, you might suppose, is a hostile element which man must overcome. But in fact, it does not work like this. On the contrary the man who is learning from his manual labour—and

---

6 Genesis 3:19

he learns by absorbing rather than by trunking it out—will tell you that he is at last coming to see what material creation is all about: he is learning of the sympathy that can exist between animate and inanimate things. As himself a work of God's hands, he is discovering an affinity with God's other works.

With his social inhibitions levelled in a larger understanding of his common humanity, with the edge of his self-interest worn down by the performance of unexciting and persevering labour, a man can discover within himself a new charity and a new peace.

In an age when people are looking for things to soothe the nerves, the practice of manual labour should have particular appeal. But in fact it seems to have very little appeal. Certainly religious, and more particularly religious of the monastic tradition, should give testimony to the healing properties, spiritual and mental, of work with the hands out of doors.

But in this, as in almost all connected with the supernatural life lived in the setting of the natural world, there can be deception and excess. We can over-simplify. We can imagine that a return to the land is the solution for everything, we can canonize husbandry, we can make an idol of rusticity, we can despise the things of the mind, we can be intolerant of those who do not follow the call which is clear enough to us, but which perhaps has never been sounded to them.

The better the idea, the more unfortunate its misconstruction. But misconstruction is accidental: it is the essence of an idea that must be grasped and followed up. Again and again it has to be insisted that it is only with the development of the life of prayer that the soul learns to distinguish between substance and accident, between the superficial and the real, between the things of absolute and relative importance.

In the case of many souls such a development is effected precisely by what we have been discussing. 'It is difficult to say whether it is in order to meditate better that they occupy themselves unceasingly in working with their hands', says Cassian of certain monks he has come across, 'or whether it is by this assiduity in labour that they acquire so much piety, knowledge, and light.'

The day of the religious is made up of prayer and work. For the monk we have seen that his prayer is twofold, private and liturgical, and that his work is twofold, reading and labor. We have seen too that the operations are mutually assisting, and that it is to prayer that everything else in the life is made subordinate.

Among the ancients the activities of the religious life, in the ascending order of their importance, were held to be: penance, labour, prayer. 'If fasting hinders your work', St Basil taught, 'it is better to eat like the workman of Christ that you are.' If work hinders your prayer—this is the teaching of St Antony to his monks in northern Egypt—then you must either learn to do it more prayerfully or give it up.[7] In Pachomian monasteries, where agriculture and crafts formed an integral part of the life, there would be no question of work being given up for prayer: prayer was assumed to be both the concomitant and end of work.

Adam before the fall was required by God, as we read in the second chapter of Genesis, to work the soil of Eden. It was no effort to him; he did it with pleasure and as an instinctive expression of homage. His body, mind, soul—that is to say his whole being—were directed to God. In our attempt to return to the state of our first parents we attempt to return to this wholeness of service.

Reading, study, and labour have been given as the most direct means towards union with God by prayer. Other direct means are of course at the individual soul's disposal, means which are taken up at the prompting of the Holy Spirit but which of necessity are not general enough to be dealt with here. Ejaculatory prayers, recognized devotions, devotions evolved out of particular customs, training, spiritual attraction: through all this the grace of God operates. Using every means we can lay hold of, whether direct or indirect, we come eventually to see, in the words of Dionysius, 'all things tending to one perfect unity under the influence of the one Holy Spirit'.

---

7 Thus to tend his garden might easily prove so distracting to a monk as to necessitate the change to a sedentary and duller occupation. Antonian monks mostly made baskets and wove linen: this was work which could be done in the cell, and was undertaken chiefly either to fill up the time that could not be spent in set prayer or the reading of Scripture; it was also, of course, a means of support.

6

THE SAFEGUARDS

IF silence is given first place among the safeguards of recollection, it is not because solitude is less important but because silence lies nearer home. Solitude is the environment which is made for the soul, or which the soul makes for itself. Silence is a question of how I keep it. 'Silence is not in the desert, nor is noise in the traffic of the bazaar.' If do not make silence, nobody else will make it for me. It must be inside me or it will be nowhere.'

If prayer is to breathe, there has to be silence in the air. Inside the soul and out, the atmosphere must be still. As always it is the inside element that is the more important of the two.

'Where silence is not observed', says Abbot Marmion, 'it can be affirmed that the inner life is lacking in intensity. Therefore our Holy Father rarely grants to his disciples the permission to speak to one another.' Certainly St Benedict attaches great weight to the *taciturnitatis gravitas*, the seriousness of silence.

We think of silence too much as the hush which results when we have managed to get rid of some particular noise. It would be better to think of it as something in its own right, as something which noise violates.

Silence should be the natural condition, the norm. It is not what comes *after* something has happened, but before. It is that which waits in tranquillity—whether for a grace, an event, or a sound. It was present in Mary before the Annunciation. It was present again in Mary throughout the time before the Nativity.

> The tranquil night
> At the approaches of the dawn,
> The silent music,
> The murmuring solitude,
> The supper which revives,
> And enkindles love.

In this stanza St John of the Cross shows the nature of true silence. For him it is the womb from which contemplation emerges; it is also the food which refreshes.

Once these two ideas of St John are grasped, silence is understood as a positive and not a negative quality. It actively co-operates in the work of prayer. Before the dawn of contemplation approaches, silence makes ready; when the soul is exhausted, silence revives it and rekindles the fires of love.

'*Et ego reficiam vos*', says our Lord. Refresh? 'Revivify' is nearer to the meaning. *Re-ficiam*—make you again, give new life to you. So, in the same way silence revivifies and re-creates the spirit. The habit of silence in the soul gives continuous renewal. There is no wastage: every grace is listened for and gently responded to.

If we are to hear the voice of the Holy Spirit in our souls, we must wait for it in silence. The Holy Spirit came down upon the apostles at Pentecost while they were waiting for it in silent retreat at the cenacle.

In yielding to the Holy Ghost, the soul yields to the gifts which further deepen its silence. The gifts of the Holy Ghost, by detaching it from the disordered appetites and drawing all its faculties into unison, disposes the soul to listen for the voice of God.

'The ears of them that hear shall hearken diligently', says Isaias, '... until the spirit be poured upon us from on high; then the desert shall be as fruitful field.' There is the silence of the desert and there is the silence of the fruitful field. The interior silence that is spiritual is not dead like a desert. Besides prayer it produces humility, fortitude, peace, joy, and insight into minds and difficulties of others.

It is not in the absence of effort, or even of struggle, that interior silence consists; it is in the absence of disorder. There will always be the need to fight temptation and to go against self: this need not disturb the silence of the soul any more than Michael's fight with Lucifer disturbed the silence of heaven.

It is order not inertia that makes for silence. It is in ordered silence that man fashions his soul so that, under grace, it comes to be what God means it to be. In silence man works out his vocation, which is to reflect God's image.

If exterior silence is to be of any value to the soul, interior silence must be its principle. And exterior silence is not so elementary as to be beneath the soul's notice. It is necessary not only to the regular and ascetical life but also to the strictly spiritual life.

Without a love of quiet, a soul will never develop in the interior life. It means detachment from variety, curiosity, and a desire to keep abreast with the interest of the moment; it also means being ruthless in suppressing the noise that comes from unnecessary entertainment.

The quiet suitable to the contemplative life is secured not only by denying excitement but also by training oneself to do things in a quiet way. The orderly behaviour required by St Benedict of his monks extends to more than the restraint which a monk should exercise when moved by powerful emotion. The *quies monastica* should both show itself and be maintained by a controlled way of moving and talking.

Obviously there can be no outward or inward silence where there is not a planned economy of speech. In *The Paradise of the Fathers* we read of Abbot Joseph asking of Abbot Nestir, 'What shall I do with my tongue, for I cannot conquer it?' 'If thou talkest,' asks Abbot Nestir in return, 'wilt thou have relief?' 'Nay,' comes the reply. 'Then if thou canst not gain relief by talking, hold thy peace.'

All monastic tradition, not merely that of the eremitical life, looks upon silence as an essential discipline for those whose vocation it is to dwell constantly upon divine things. But it would be a mistake for monks to think of silence as a penance; rather they should think of it as a happiness and enjoy it. Silence becomes a continuous burden to a monk only if it is constantly broken.

'What shall I do?' a novice asked Abbot Bessarion. The old man answered, 'Keep silence, and consider thyself to be nothing.' If, as the result of our silence, we consider ourselves to be something, we must know that we are not keeping silence properly. Silence, besides being a means to recollection, is a means to humility.

Whatever the religious order, solitude in some degree is necessary to the religious. The more active the work, the more sedulous must be the individual religious in cultivating the spirit of solitude.

The soul that has a love of silence will see to it that the conditions of solitude are fulfilled and maintained. Silence, interior quiet, is the principle of abstraction and withdrawal. The negative derives its character from the positive.

But it is only the outward features of solitude that suggest the negative: its separations are only half its function. There is power in solitude; like silence, it is not a vacuum but a force.

If we think of solitude as life in a lonely void, we think mistakenly. It is not an emptiness but a plenitude. The solitude of a man of prayer is filled with the presence of God.

Just as speech that comes out from distraction and dissipation is vapid, the speech that comes out from true solitude is real and wise. Solitude safeguards judgment as well as silence and recollection.

The centre of our solitude is not the point furthest from the lines which mark our separation from the world; the centre of our solitude is in our own souls. It is not in the geographical setting that we shall find what we are looking for, but in our spiritual setting. The kingdom of God is within us.

So long as we look upon solitude in terms either of physical aloneness or of negation we are liable to be held captive by the superficial. We must look upon it as the seed-ground of graces, as something which brings the spiritual life to harvest and maturity.

Far from being a negation, it is an affirmation: it speaks to us immediately of God. But it must be of God that it speaks and not of the picturesque. There can be glamour about solitude. There is a lure of loneliness that is wrong: we must not make a cult of being solitary. For the love of God, a man may be solitary—may even have to be lonely— but he must assure himself that this is his true reason for seeking solitude.

'To please God alone' is the reason St Benedict looks for in the man who applies for admission to the monastery. Not to please his sense of the dramatic, or even to please those whom he hopes to join. He comes in order to live to God alone. In joining a community of cenobites, he does not come to live as a hermit; nevertheless he comes to live alone to God.

Of St Benedict himself St Gregory wrote that 'he dwelt in that solitude alone, keeping himself continually in the sight of his Creator… as often as by the fervour of contemplation he was elevated, he left himself as it were beneath.'

There are degrees in separation from the world, but there is no degree in the life of recollection which is proposed to the individual religious: each is called to be completely recollected.

Whatever the work given to the soul, whatever the nature of its obligations as a religious of a particular order, solitude is neither an extra, a luxury, an affectation, nor a burden. It is an environment which has to be built up and defended. We have quoted St John of the Cross in connection with silence, we can quote another stanza of his here. He speaks of the bride:

> In solitude she lived,
> And in solitude she built her nest;
> And in solitude alone
> Hath the Beloved guided her,
> In solitude also wounded with love.

The lines to note especially are those which say that it was only in solitude that she was guided by the Beloved.

Just as solitude, the physical kind, goes far towards insuring silence and recollection, so enclosure goes far towards insuring solitude. Enclosure does not guarantee solitude, but it promotes and defends it.

Just as you cannot bring silence in a sealed tank into a room full of people talking, so you cannot bring solitude into the religious life unless there is some of it there already. The religious life makes provision for it with its rules of enclosure.

The point of religious enclosure, then, is to see that a measure of actual solitude exists in which the individual soul may build up a spirit of solitude.

Unless enclosure produces in the religious an effect of wanting to co-operate with the graces of the interior life, it serves no useful purpose. Unless it is seen as ministering to recollection, it is no more than a matter of boundaries.

If the essence of enclosure does not consist in the walls which surround it, neither does it consist in the penalties attached to breaking it. The spirit of recollection that depended upon fear of neglecting its safeguards would not be strong enough to carry the soul to union with God.

In the last analysis it is not the safeguards that the soul must lean upon; the soul must lean upon God. All that the safeguards can do is to defend the things which make it easier for the soul to lean continually upon God.

Thus, enclosure should not be thought of as confining to a certain area, but rather as bringing greater liberty: the soul is made free to dwell longer and more deeply in God.

If enclosure is leant on as an end in itself, it becomes an eccentricity. Man can make an idol out of almost anything. He can debase something useful and good so that it becomes not only useless but bad.

By forgetting the purpose of enclosure, a man may make either a fetish or an insupportable burden of it. Enclosure is designed to be something better than a fad and more helpful than a millstone.

One of the features which distinguish the monastic from other religious orders is the conception of enclosure. In an earlier chapter we have seen how St Benedict contrives to shelter his monks from unnecessary contact with the outside world. It is for the individual monk to see how far he falls in with the mind of his holy father.

If St Benedict goes to the length of ruling that his monasteries should be built and equipped as self-contained units ('so that there may be no need for the monks to go about outside, since it is not at all good for their souls'), if he makes it the exception for monks to be allowed out, if he insists that certain conditions should be observed on the occasions when leaving the enclosure is a necessity (conditions relating to meals, prayers, and time-table), if the returning monk is required to ask the whole community to pray that his soul may be purified from whatever harmful image he may have carried in from the world, and if all discussion of news picked up while away is forbidden, then that Benedictine is inexcusable, whatever period he belongs to in the history of monasticism, who pretends that there is no issue at stake.

A man has only to read the Holy Rule to see what things St Benedict felt to be important. Conditions may have altered, the Church's needs may have brought in new approaches, the principles which St Benedict stood for may have had to be interpreted in their changed social or psychological or economic context, but when all allowances have been made it still remains true that enclosure is an integral part of the Benedictine ideal.

Obviously St Benedict's concept of enclosure cannot be realized by those of his followers whose particular vocation it is to take directly into account the needs of society. Already in St Gregory's time the difficulty of combining the two ideals was evident. So much so that this great monastic pope was forced to admit that 'No one can at the same time devote himself to ecclesiastical duties and observe wholly the monastic rule; it would be impossible for him who is daily involved in Church affairs to keep to the regularity of the monastery.'

Nevertheless, every religious, whether or not obliged by the Rule of St Benedict and whatever his or her commitment to external work, should have to form some sort of ideal of seclusion. However narrow the confines of the particular enclosure, the religious of every order or congregation will surely have something in the way of defined separation from the world to be faithful to.

Certainly, for the monk there must be respect for the principle which in fact may be impossible of fulfilment. Obedience is more important than enclosure, and if he has to leave his seclusion at the will of his superior, he more than makes up in virtue what he has lost in maintaining an observance. But though obedience may have reduced both the area of his enclosure and the time which he is allowed to spend in it, a monk must know that his reasons for leaving it on his own initiative, and with all permissions, must be very good reasons indeed.

For example, the common good, individual necessity, *contemplata aliis tradere*,[1] requirements of study or the learning of a craft or trade which will benefit the community: these things would justify waiving the idea of enclosure in deference to a greater or a more immediate good. Boredom with the routine, desire to see places and people, impulse, desire to avoid people and duties: these would not.

It should be noted, before the subject is left, that the question of enclosure has two approaches: the door of the gate-house can be opened from the inside or from the outside. The spirit of enclosure is threatened not only by what is allowed to leave it, but by what is allowed to enter it.

After taking all that trouble to leave the world and set limits to this enclave of religion, it would be folly to invite the world to come and share the joys of isolation.

Guests will never be wanting to a monastery, and they are to be received as Christ Himself would be received. Indeed, the apostolate of a monastery can be largely expressed in its dealings with externs who present themselves as visitors. But there is a difference between entertaining people as souls and entertaining them as men of the world, between looking for Christ in them and looking in them for someone who will be either a good listener or a good talker. Always it has to be remembered that those inside and those outside the religious state, each from their particular angle, are witnesses to Christ and to His love.

Lastly, as a safeguard to recollection, and to the spirit of peace generally in the religious life, there is the support of religious poverty. Less directly than the defences enumerated, poverty helps no less really: it enables the soul, by insisting that full trust is placed in God's Providence and not in material goods and prospects, to free itself of a hundred anxieties which otherwise would distract its prayer.

The *Introit* of the Mass for the feast of St Benedict Joseph Labre

---

[1] To hand over contemplations to others.

reads as follows: 'I have left my house, I have renounced my inheritance; I am needy and poor, but the Lord has picked me up.' The text is composed from two psalms and a verse in the prophecy of Jeremias. The idea is the same as that expressed in the canticle of Moses: 'He carried him on His shoulders; God alone was his guide.'

Poverty then, like enclosure, is liberative; but only to the soul that expects the Lord to pick it up, only to the soul whose only guide is God Given this confidence, the soul finds itself shedding temporal cares and able to yield to the direction of the Holy Spirit.

Poverty, then, like solitude, is a positive quality and carries a positive promise: 'Blessed are the poor in spirit, for theirs is the kingdom of heaven.' But again, there is an implied condition: the poverty has to be lived for the love of God. Without the supernatural direction the good of poverty is likely to be wasted. As in the case of cleanness of heart, if the virtue of it came naturally our Lord would not have made it a beatitude.

The very framing of the beatitude, the whole of it set in the present tense, confirms the assertion that poverty is one of the chief safeguards to prayer. 'Theirs is the kingdom of heaven': in anticipation, that is in prayer and in faith, the poor of spirit already possess the goal of their desire.

7
EFFECTS

NOT only are the effects of prayer upon the soul beyond estimation, but even if numerically they could be accounted for—and this would require a book in itself—the individual soul would appear in whom prayer had produced individual results. Accordingly, we confine ourselves to the consideration of the most general effects; particular manifestations are more the matter for specialized study or autobiography.

Men have said of almost every human ill that it can be overcome by one or another power with which rational beings are endowed. Nearly always they give primacy to the human will. Fear, doubt, loneliness: the human will can apparently crush these things down. It is a comforting doctrine, but what if I do not happen to possess such a masterful will?

If it is not the will it is the intellect. Reason can see the folly of worrying, of trying to find an absolute answer to human problems, of seeking happiness in material possessions. This is all very nice, but what if my mind can grasp so little of philosophy that worry and doubt still persist?

To deal with loneliness and frustration, we are further told, there is the ever-developing science of psychology that we can draw upon.

What we need is a deeper knowledge of our temperaments, and the willingness to make certain readjustments. But what if, after all the help that psychology can give me, my temperament is still a mystery to me and refuses to be pinned down?

This preamble is not leading up to the assertion that the life of prayer can do all that the combined powers of character-training, philosophy, and psychology can claim to do. It is to suggest that by approaching the human problem from another angle, the prayer angle, a soul will have less need to rely upon what can be taught by man, and that the evils of doubt, fear, loneliness, frustration and so on are not so much fought and conquered as acknowledged and transcended.

Since everything in the spiritual life should be leading the soul to a closer appreciation of the realities of faith, it follows that where grace is faithfully responded to, a habit of mind is acquired which is not earthly but heavenly. The soul, that is, comes to see things from above.

The same things are there that were there before—the soul may even have to suffer more in the way of fear, doubt, loneliness, and frustration—but they will be met out of different reserves. Instead of having to school myself in courage, I shall offer my dread to God in trust. Within the doubt I shall, while groping painfully and feeling hopelessly unconvinced, make acts of faith. With loneliness and frustration it will be the same: surrender to the will of God which must somehow be their explanation.

Thus, it is not strictly that as a result of prayer in his life a man becomes immune where he was vulnerable before. It is that he does not expect to get over his difficulties by any natural means whatever. He sees the whole thing as planned by God, in whose hands alone lies the remedy.

To the soul of prayer, the one absolute reality is the will of God. Nothing else is of any consequence. It is easy then to see how simplified, say for the saint, the range of evils becomes. The one thing that the saint dreads above all is offending God: other fears are relative and can be treated lightly. Doubt? The sense of isolation and not belonging? Failure, baulked hopes? Where such things are understood solely in reference to God they are dealt with in the spirit and not in the flesh.

No matter how over-sensitive a soul may be by nature, by grace he can be made to endure. He does not have to will himself into a high heroism; all he has to do is to accept the particular pressure of the moment and submit his sensitive nature to the unifying and strengthening action of the Holy Spirit. The impressionable, shrinking, nervous temperament is taken up by the power of God and made into a new thing. Not that it becomes suddenly forthright and robust; rather it becomes gradually the instrument and channel of the Holy Spirit, its very sensitiveness telling now in its favour.

If the whole prayer-life consists in the uniting of the human personality with the divine, we must come more and more to a settled harmony within ourselves. For as long as we live on earth there will always be conflicts, always be a longing to escape and find peace, but there is such a thing as the tranquillity of faith. In our insecurity, we rest secure in God.

It is His security rather than ours that is the stuff of our peace. Where the human will coincides with the divine will whatever there is of shrinking and nerves and sadness is superficial: disgust and melancholy are the last protest of the emotions. The emotions, when crossed, are a truculent lot.

Fluctuating between joy and sorrow, hope and despair, the soul is all the time being drawn into a unity which is so deep-seated as to escape recognition on the surface. We see only the opposing forces at work, we feel only the tension of divided desire and the uncertainty of the issue, but so long as we can say in the will, 'This is what God wants, so I want it also,' there is no conflict at the level which signifies.

The primary effect of prayer, then, is simply this, that the soul sees life as a whole, as a unity, as a single expression of God's will. Its own movement towards God is seen as the movement of God within Himself. Its own perfection, its own suffering, happiness, effort, prayer, work: all this is so much more the work of God than its own work that self fades out of the picture and only God remains.

It is not that the soul decides to avoid introspection as a waste of time and energy; it is that introspection is replaced by the inner attraction of God. This attraction—though the soul may not see it as such, indeed may not see it at all—is in fact the attraction of God to Himself.

Light is making itself felt, but not as before. Hitherto the light of grace shone upon self within the soul, and upon the affairs of self; now it shines upon God within the soul, and upon the affairs of God. Thus it is God who enlightens and who is revealed. He is at once the agent and the acted-on, the seeker and the sought.

As a consequence of this general effect of prayer, a number of further effects follow. The soul finds itself revising some of its assumptions, shedding some of its complications, and practising interiorly and without difficulty some of the virtues which up till now have been found difficult enough to practise outwardly.

Thus, for example, viewed from this new level which sees human affairs in closer relation to the divine and therefore more comprehensively, the cross is appreciated in a new way. It is understood, not as a sign of division, but as the sign of union; not as the stretching of humanity to fit the form of divinity, but as the drawing of the physical into its true and proper shape.

The cross is a stumbling-block to the Jews and foolishness to the Gentiles, but to those who see in the light of truth, whether Jews or Greeks, Christ crucified is the power and the wisdom of God. Surely what St Paul is telling the Corinthians is that they must not be *surprised* by the cross: it is the most normal thing in the world.

Thus, to the soul of prayer the cross is no shock. Pain, misunderstanding, failure, violence: none of these will be spared the man of prayer. But the man of prayer will know that each is fitting and right and true. The cross is not incongruous; it exactly matches the pattern.

While the shape of the cross may symbolize a tearing apart, it may also, by its outstretched arms, suggest the most characteristic attitude of love. Suffering is part of man's worship; but not the whole part. On the cross Christ took up the position of a lover as well as that of a victim.

In this larger and more inclusive understanding of the cross the soul comes to a larger and more inclusive understanding of renunciation. Mortification is felt to be something more than giving up superfluities; the essence of it is seen as giving in to God.

Where the soul has turned fully towards God there is no need to work out a system of mortification. The reason for this is that the soul has turned away from creatures. We tend to begin from the wrong end, the end which lays stress on what has to be renounced, and so are discouraged at the very outset.

If we proposed to ourselves the life of prayer and the love of God, mortification would follow as second nature. We would not have to tear ourselves free from creatures; creatures would either drop away of their own accord or else become assimilated into the spiritual scene.

Thus, to the soul of prayer the question of mortification virtually solves itself. If my selfhood is uprooted and handed over to God, the leaves of unnecessary concessions in the way of luxury go with the rest of the tree.

Where the soul may at first have been held back from the complete surrender to God—saying, 'I shall never bring myself to the point of giving up cigarettes'—it now, having discovered the power of prayer and the life of love, does not bother about the list of things which have to be discarded.

The soul that really 'launches out into the deep' in faith and love will find that whatever cargo it came away with will fall overboard. One by one the items of freight will be shed, and the soul will be drawn on its course feeling lighter.

There are many who, longing all the time to launch out into the open sea, paddle their over-loaded craft in the shallows by the shore. It is not so much that the cargo is too heavy but that they are too hesitant. They see this pile of accumulated possessions, self-indulgences, useless ambitions, idle regrets, scruples, unruly affections, antipathies, and they say, 'I dare not put out to sea like that.' They look wistfully at the horizon, and then steer closer inland again.

What such souls need is a second, or third, or fourth 'conversion': they need to 'turn to' God with their whole being in prayer. If they keep their faces towards God, they will learn to trust. Conversion means turning *to* as much as it means turning *from*.

As in the field of mortification, so in every other department of the spiritual life: prayer simplifies, expands, penetrates to the inward significance. The practical judgment, enlightened by its contact with the supernatural, becomes spiritual discernment. The will to succeed, purified of selfish motive, becomes supernatural zeal. The affective powers, given a new momentum, are directed through natural objects to find rest solely in God.

So it is also in the natural virtues: hospitality does not stop short at being amiable to friends; integrity means something new and much more comprehensive; justice looks to the real need and the supernatural end rather than to the fairest thing to be done under the circumstances. In prayer the soul learns new valuations and applies them instinctively. The soul goes to work with a sureness born of possessing the mind of Christ within itself.

The soul knows at last, and experimentally, that its acts of virtue are elicited by grace. 'I have nothing of my own that I can boast of', the soul can say with absolute conviction, 'everything is lent to me for my use. At every moment I am being given strength from God to fight temptation, to persevere, to suffer. If I am called upon to make decisions, it is His wisdom that decides through me. Where help is asked of me, it is His help that goes out to others through what I, as His instrument, say to them or do for them. Not even my prayers are my own: they are what He does, praying in me.'

In this way humility is learned without being studied. It is expressed without being formulated. No credit is taken for it by the soul, because it is seen to be the humility of Christ communicating itself.

In attempting to live the Christ-life, the soul reduplicates, in its degree, the virtues of Christ. Patience, charity, endurance, gentleness: prayer, in uniting the soul with the prototype of virtue, gives access to all these. Whether or not the accession is appreciated by the soul does not matter: if no merit is appropriated to itself, the soul is not harmed by the knowledge.

'He that is mighty has done great things to me', our Lady was able to say in perfect humility.[1] Equally objective is the statement of St Paul: 'His grace in me has not been void ... by His grace I am what I am.'[2]

---

1 Luke 1:49
2 1 Corinthians 15:10

How else, except by claiming for them this de-selfed acknowledgment of grace operating within, explain the abiding humility of the saints in the face of their evident sanctity? To the saints themselves no explanation is ever needed. Their prayer has taught them to assume that their sanctity is not their own.

To us who are not saints such assumptions do not come readily. Always we have to be reminding ourselves that sanctity is, not what we achieve, but what is achieved by Christ in us. We do not make progress by our own labour but by the labour of God. We do not arrive at perfect love by our own power to love, but by God's power to love.

The miraculous, the heroic, the mystical: these things may be matters of wonder to the saints, but they are not, as they are to us, matters of surprise. The saint lives in a different dimension, the dimension of faith. It is the grace of prayer that brings the soul closer to the saint's focus of vision—as it is prayer that has brought the saint closer to Christ's.

In the increased simplicity of outlook which prayer develops in the soul, the hundred unresolved questions which have been bothering the mind for years are transcended. It is not that they become easier to understand; it is that they become easier to accept. They do not bother the mind any more; they are not a distraction.

This affects not only mysteries of faith but problems of experience. The soul no longer speculates as to whether, for example, love is proved by suffering or suffering is proved by love: the soul simply takes its sufferings in its stride and loves all it can without asking further.

The soul does not trouble itself as to whether, for example, it would love more if it knew more: it simply tries to love more, and in doing so finds that it comes to know more. All questions seem to reduce themselves to the one question, and the one question is very simply answered.

Perhaps the most curious of the effects of the prayer-life upon the soul, and certainly the most difficult one to describe so that it makes sense, is the state of mind which combines isolation of spirit with the conviction of being incorporated with others. The soul, while conscious of being an exile, is conscious also of belonging.

At one and the same time the soul feels painfully estranged from God, from its fellow human beings, from any sort of happiness which might be found either in God or in creatures, and yet feels that all this must be right and meant. It feels that this is its only way of being united to God and united to humanity.

The soul does not understand, but it knows. It knows that if the seed must die in order to live, then the soul is most united when it is most separated. The one text to which the soul clings at this stage is, 'My God, My God, why hast Thou forsaken Me?' The soul knows that Father and Son were never for one instant apart.

Thus, in the last analysis the effect of the prayer-life is a deepening of faith. The soul believes that despite all contrary evidence God has not left it forever. It hopes and it loves. The hopes may have to be indefinitely deferred, and the acts of love may seem to be without meaning or value, but all the time the virtue of trust, proved in the soul's surrender, is being brought out. With St John of the Cross the soul cries out in its longing:

> ... Thou wilt show me
> That which my soul desired;
> And there Thou wilt give me at once,
> O Thou, my life,
> That which Thou gavest me the other day.

The longing is, unknown to the soul, the proof of its love. Felt possession is not the proof of love; the longing of faith is the proof of love.

BOOK III
THE YOKE OF COMMUNITY LIFE

1
COMMON AIM

IN the first book we saw that the aim proposed in the religious life is the perfection of charity; in the second we examined one aspect of charity, namely the love of God as expressed in prayer; we come now, in the third and last book, to consider charity as expressed towards others in religion.

This is not to suggest that the religious is free to choose between prayer and fraternal charity; it is rather to insist that fraternal charity confirms the love expressed in prayer, while prayer preserves the supernatural character of conventual life.

The man of prayer is not so wrapped up in the love of God that he has no love left over for his brethren; rather he has so enlarged his capacity of love by loving God that he has all the more room for the love of others.

The man of prayer is not so cut off from creatures by his renunciation of them that he is indifferent to their need; rather he is so detached from the false good which is to be found in creatures that he is all the more truly related to them at a level where both their own need and his can be met.

In the same way the man of fraternal charity is not so committed to his brethren as to have no time left over for God; rather he sees God so clearly in His creatures that he knows how vital it is to preserve this vision of reality by means of assiduous prayer.

Ideally speaking, then, the two aspects of charity make common cause. The soul should be able to pass, without making any wrench of the mind, from the presence of God in people to the presence of God in prayer. The love that is learned in prayer finds its appropriate expression in community life.

Thus, the religious who works towards a separatist charity is working towards a vacuum. By concentrating solely on either the love of God or the love of man a soul will find himself unsupported between the two. The first thing which he has to learn about love is that it is not exclusive but inclusive. The love of Christ is all-embracing. Nothing is outside its range except sin.

As Christians we are under the obligation of loving one another as Christ has loved us. Nothing could be more comprehensive; nothing could be stated more clearly. As a religious I am more than ever under the obligation of this charity which is Christ's.

I may find solitude more congenial than the company of my brethren, or again I may prefer their society to the loneliness of my cell: either way I must express charity. I may not evade the implication of charity in any direction.

You may say that the affective nature of man is so fashioned as to lay hold only of the good and the true, and that where these qualities are wanting in the objects presented to man's charity there can be no claim upon his love. If then, it is in the very nature of man to love only what is lovable, how, you may ask, can a man in religion (or anywhere else) be expected to love people who are neither good nor true?

The answer is simply that since God loves all men, men must do so too. 'As Christ has loved us.' The unlovable and the untrue are forgotten in the act of love. The element of good in every man is so infinitely more significant that love can form the bond.

The image of God may be overlaid, but in every soul it must be there. God made the soul precisely because of this likeness to Himself. He loves the soul precisely for what He sees of this likeness in the soul. So, when we speak of 'loving God in human beings' we speak of something which God does. Just as He does it, so also must we.

But note that we love the likeness, not the unlikeness. We do not love in our brethren the features which bear no resemblance to God. We do not love their bad moods, their imperfections, their un-Christlike behaviour: we love the brethren themselves. We do not love their characters as such—any more than we love their taste as such or their views as such—but we love them as reflections of God.

Loving their souls, we must love their progress in sanctity. It is here that we begin to see that the aim of the religious life is a common aim, and that the religious must mutually assist one another in its direction.

There is the perfection of the individual religious and there is the perfection of the religious community. They are different perfections, but they interact one upon another. The community that has the spirit of God will spur the individual soul towards perfection; the soul that has the spirit of God will influence the community in the same way. But though it is true to say that the community finds its perfection in the sanctity of the members, it would not be true to say that the members find their perfection in the sanctity of the community. The members find perfection in nothing else but in perfectly fulfilling the will of God.

But at once it must be added that for the members of a community the will of God *is* that they co-operate in the work of the whole. The end of their endeavour may not be the glorification of their house, but in their endeavour to give glory to God the individual members must be vividly aware of their responsibility to its spirit.

Each individual member, by responding to his particular call of grace, contributes to the spiritual good of his community. But the call of grace is not the same for each member. Say you have a community of twenty religious, all striving after perfection, you get one ideal but twenty different interpretations.

The sanctity proposed by the religious life is the sanctity of Christ. Christ is undivided, 'the same yesterday, today, and forever'.[1] But each soul sees this sanctity differently, through the lens of his own personality. Christ presents Himself to your twenty religious in His way, and each soul responds to the ideal in his own way.

---

1   Hebrews 13:8

Consequently, in no religious community will there be an identical spirituality followed by all. The spirituality would be suspect if there were. Such uniformity would imply that a form had been superimposed from without. Spirituality works upwards from within, not downwards and by dictation.

The spirituality of a soul is the direct work of grace; the spirituality of a community is the work of grace too, but operating through the spirituality of the individual religious.

The spirit of the community is one thing, the spirituality of the individual soul is another. A community may enjoy the grace of a truly monastic spirit which an individual monk may entirely miss; a monk may be leading a deeply interior life in a community which has either lost or never found true spirituality.

The spirit of a community depends upon a number of influences; some of these are external, some are internal; some are inherited from the past, others emerge out of existing circumstances. The spirituality of a community is both more independent of influence and more specific in kind. As in the case of the individual soul, spirituality is either there or not there. Once there, it admits of degree—like any other quality it may be more pronounced or less—but so far as its range of interest goes, its sole object is God.

If true spirituality does not mean stereotyped spirituality, true monastic spirit does not mean stereotyped monastic spirit. The monastic ideal is set before twenty monks, not before twenty automatons. Among these brethren of common purpose and common charity there will never be an identity of view regarding monastic policy and interpretation. It might even, again, be a bad sign if there were.

In the case of any social unit the vigour of its life depends, not upon regimentation, but upon the harmonious working of divers elements: even of divergent elements. Without an exchange of different ideas, without the interaction of differing opinions, the intellectual organism dies. Where the social unit is also a religious unit a closer attention may have to be paid to the necessity of harmony in operation, but the same law applies.

Whatever the variety or conformity of view among the members, charity remains always the community ideal. For each soul, as for the whole body, the end of the religious life is love.

What we have been discussing above is the difference of understanding, not the conflict of wills. It is no sign of health where the diversity of interpretation disturbs the harmony of charity.

Charity remains always the absolute. Departure from charity in the religious life shows up the false spirituality, the partisan view, the bitter zeal. Common purpose is preserved only where there is common submission in common charity.

The test lies in the submission. The test of a monk's religious spirit does not lie in the loftiness of his views but in the surrender of his will.

It is no good having strict principles if the principles happen to be wrong. It is no good practising exact fidelity to schedule if the schedule happens to be not exactly the one which God wants practised. It is no good looking for a sanctity which is outside the limitations imposed by grace.

The one test which covers every contingency is submission of the will. That is why obedience and charity go together in the religious life. The monk who surrenders his own private views of monasticism for the sake of the common good is practising obedience and charity at the same time.

If grace does not enable the soul to alter its judgment, it enables the soul to immolate its judgment. While the soul may, with the best will in the world, find itself incapable of surrendering its opinions in the sense of denying them, it will find itself able to surrender them in the sense of sacrificing them.

A soul sacrifices the judgment by silencing the expressions of the judgment. So long as the will is surrendered, the opinions which lie in the judgment have neither more nor less power to do damage than the emotions which lie in the heart.

To silence the judgment, as to silence the emotions, may be to practise heroic obedience and high charity. When the monk has sacrificed everything else, he will find there is still scope for sacrifice in the matter of his opinions. Certainly it is the best proof of his humility.

Thus, in submission to the common will, which is the substance of community life, is to be found the combined good of charity, obedience and humility. In his Easter sermons, St Bernard has much to say on surrendering the personal will and judgment to the common will and judgment. His argument is that personal ideas, however well attested, are always liable to be tainted with self-love. For him the only safety lies in letting Christ so live in the soul as to will through the soul.

The soul in whom, and through whom, Christ wills is defended against the excesses of self-will and self-love. Such a soul now wills in charity, wills according to the common will and towards the common good.

'We must buy with the money of our own will', says St Bernard, 'for when we lose our own will we lose nothing; nay rather we gain much, disposing of it for something better since what was individual becomes common. *For love is common will.* We buy without price when we receive what we had not, and retain more securely what we had. How will he sympathize with a brother who of his own will knows only how to feel for himself?'

Selfishness narrows the soul to the limits of its own experience; charity expands it to the limitless experience of common humanity.

Self-will, in order to attain its own good, overrides the good of others and even the greater glory of God. Its sole criterion is its own desire. 'Let only self-will cease, and there will be no hell; for against what will does that fire rage but against self-will?' It is the *voluntas propria* in the soul which fights against the *voluntas informata* which has accepted the direction of faith.[2]

Even more dangerous than the *voluntas propria*, says St Bernard, is the soul's *proprium consilium*. (Flower translates this as 'self-confidence' but it surely means private judgment or personal opinion.) It is more dangerous because it is more secret. 'It is the leprosy of those who have a zeal for God, but not according to knowledge. They follow their own error, and are so obstinate in it that they will not listen to the advice of any. These are the breakers of unity and the enemies of peace.'

Pursuing a course of *propria voluntas* and *proprium consilium* the soul separates itself from both God and the brethren. Obstinacy en-

---

2 'Self-will' and 'well-formed will'.

trenches it against the one thing which could bring relief and rescue—the common will.

'Who does not now blush to be obstinate in his own opinion', asks St Bernard, 'since the very Wisdom gave up His? He so changed His opinion that He put off until His thirtieth year that upon which He had already entered.'

The monk, by surrendering in charity and faith to the common will of the community, finds his own sanctity in the sanctity of others. He is not compromising with an alien spirit; he is conforming to the common spirit of Christ and His members. He is not making concessions in a mood of patronage; he is emptying himself in the terms of Christ's abjection.

Where the good, or the imagined good, of self is passed over in favour of the good of the community, the point of focus is not only brought out into the open but is carried up into the heights of love. The good desired is now objective and real and inevitably supernatural, instead of subjective and supposed and largely mixed up with the natural. Common good means common spiritual good or it means nothing.

If common good meant natural well-being—still more if it meant material well-being—the same obligation would not exist. But it means the supernatural destiny of the whole and the consequent glory to God. For the soul to turn aside from this would be to find bitterness and loneliness where it looked for sanctity. Such a religious life would be no life at all; it would be apart from the divine life, and so would be death.

This act of subordinating personal will and opinion to the will and opinion of the community, and to do so not out of laziness but in the name of religious charity, is a voluntary and a supernatural act. It results not from any necessity of fact but from the impulse of charity. Charity is the *terminus a quo* and *ad quem*.[3]

As such the act does in effect very closely reflect the act by which Christ 'emptied Himself, taking upon Him the form of a servant'.[4] It was His charity towards us, as St Bernard (this time in his sermons

---

3   End to which and to what.
4   Philippians 2:7

on the Canticle) points out, that prompted Christ's humility. His act of submission to the common will was not an enforced act. 'He was able to appear vile and abject in the eyes of men without thinking Himself to be so, for He knew Himself well.'

Knowing Himself to be above all, Christ humbled Himself to be below all. It was not the verdict of truth or the force of events or the ruling of human authority that caused Christ to forgo his rights. It was love.

'This kind of voluntary humility', says St Bernard, 'is not produced in us by the logical power of truth, but is created within us by the inpouring of charity; it comes from the heart, the affections, the will.'

In co-operating with the mind of his community a monk is dying to himself and living to others. Denying his own zeal, he is a zealous monk; smothering his own devotion he is stirring the devotion of others; tearing up his own plans he is furthering the plan of God.

Without a living faith it is all too easy to stop short at the common will and to forget what the common will is aiming at. The common will has meaning and value only because it wills the will of God. If it does not do this it is useless, and if it does it *is* the will of God.

If it were not God's will that religious should sink themselves in the common life and purpose of the community, He would not call them to join the community. He would not cause monasteries to be formed, nor would He provide the graces necessary for the cenobitical life to be led.

But since He has done all this for the religious life as a whole and for the members of it in particular, the aim is clear: religious acquiesce in their corporate endeavour, and in doing so acquiesce in the divine conclusion to their work. In this is fulfilled the twofold demand of charity. It is the perfect life outlined in the Gospel; it is the life of Christ Himself.

2

COMMON PRINCIPLE

WE have just seen that in fulfilling our purpose as monks living together in community we are given for our example the subjection of Christ's will to the will of others. In the present chapter we are to see that Christ is not our pattern only, but also the principle of our life, thought, and action.

This is to say that His presence in our community obligation is more than an outward influence, a form to which we con-form and according to which, when we have departed from it, we re-form ourselves; it is the essential inspiration, the very source and motive of our fraternal charity.

A model is something separate from the person who models. The model is there as a help. It is not the principal agent. Christ is our model in the sense that He proposes Himself for our imitation: we fashion ourselves according to the pattern which He has given to us. But in the process of modelling, the relationship is infinitely closer than the terms of the analogy would allow. Here Christ is not separate, outside the soul. Here Christ is the principal agent. Here the model is all, and the one who models is having his eyes and fingers trained from within.

It is the growth in us of Christ's own love both for the brethren and for ourselves that causes us to exercise our community virtues.

This does not mean that we are passive spectators, regarding with bemused wonder the multiplication of our good qualities: it means that, actively co-operating, we acknowledge with gratitude the source of that power which makes even fallen nature capable of reflecting the qualities of Christ.

We show ourselves to be tolerant, forgiving, loyal, ready to help, ready to recreate or labour with one another, ready to sympathize or congratulate *only* in so far as we are united to Christ and drawing our strength from Him. Otherwise all this is purely natural.

If I fulfil my duty towards the brethren merely because I have an academic interest in traditional forms of cenobitic life, I may be a good historian or a good actor; I am not a good monk.

Unless Christ's virtue is the principle of my response to the challenge of community life—as it must be of my renunciation, my prayer, my perseverance, and everything else about my vocation—I am merely floating on the surface. I am missing the essence of the life, the deep thing, and am amusing myself with the patterns in the foam.

Though in living the Christ-life I may go back in mind from my here-and-now monastic life to find precedent for my decisions and action in the life of Christ as recorded for me in the Gospel, I am not engaging myself thereby in an antiquarian or textual experiment. It is largely upon what I know of the historical figure that my interior knowledge of Christ depends.

To know Christ and to live the life of Christ, I must know about Christ and live according to His spoken word. But if my knowledge of Christ and my reproduction of His life are limited to what has come to me from sources outside myself, I know and live incompletely. The sacramental system exists for the purpose of making the Christ-life a reality in human souls.

Without the life of grace, begotten in us by baptism, we would still be able to read the books of the New Testament. But without grace how far would our reading get us? It is only the light of the Holy Spirit, which is Christ's Spirit, that shows us the essential Christ.

The accounts of our Lord's life preserved for us by the evangelists, the tradition of the early Church, the Holy Rule, the whole history of the religious life throughout the centuries: they all point to one thing only—the central mystery of the Christian life, Christ Himself.

Not only does everything point to Christ, as a beam of light directed in the dark shows up a statue, but Christ is in the act both of pointing and of recognition. He is the light of the world, directing His own light which shines upon Himself.

The Christian life is nothing else but Christ; the monastic life is nothing else but Christ. The requirements for the Christian and for the monk are in substance the same; the difference lies only in the particular kind of stress that is given to them.

The Church exists so that souls should lead the life of Christ; the monastery exists for the same purpose. Whether it is union with Him in the world or in the cloister, it is union that is the soul's purpose. Nothing else matters but this. All else is relative, all else must be considered as means. Union in charity is the whole end of man. God is the only absolute.

Having abstracted from the accidental and brought ourselves before the essential, we might easily make the mistake of living in an imaginary world of negations and abstractions. But the Christian ideal has to be worked out on earth before it is crowned in heaven.

In the same way the monastic ideal has to be lived out in monasteries. There is nothing supra-rational about the community life. It is transcendental only in the sense that it is supernaturally orientated. Charity is an eminently practical affair.

The monastic ideal is both tested and realized in the immediate reality. The norm or setting is the present, concrete, geographical place. It is as prosaic and realistic as that.

In order to find reality I may have to abstract, but reality does not lie in abstractions. An ideal, if it is a real one, cannot be altogether an abstraction. It cannot even rest on abstractions.

The validity of my process of abstraction is tested by my handling of actuality. The monastic life as lived by me in this monastery in the present century is what lies under the microscope. This, so far as I am affected and made responsible, is the verification of my Christian and monastic ideals. I am my own most telling commentary on the Gospel and on the rule.

From the idea of Christ as the principle both of monasticism in general and of the individual monk's practice and perfection, the idea naturally suggests itself of Christ revealing Himself in the contacts of the brethren living together.

Since He is in each of us, we must recognize Christ in others, besides ourselves. Indeed, it is better that we should concentrate on the Christ-life in others. If we lay too much stress upon the Christ-life in ourselves we are apt to think too much about ourselves and not enough about others. Which would mean that we were getting the Christ-life wrong.

If we think of union with God only in terms of prayer, and not also in terms of charity, we are back again at the error of isolationism. It is our business, not only as men of charity but as men of prayer, to forget about ourselves as much as possible.

The self-forgetting virtues are the most difficult of all to acquire. Only the truly Christlike attain to either selfless prayer or selfless charity. Certainly nothing but the direct operation of grace can separate the soul from self-interest.

But where grace is responded to, and where the temptation to self-examination is resisted, the soul moves forward and outward to Christ in an increasingly objective spirituality. There is nothing in this to suggest a return to the sense-appreciation of His presence such as might be enjoyed in the exercise of discursive prayer. Nor does it mean that the soul ceases to think of Christ as dwelling within. It means, quite simply, that the soul thinks more of Christ and less of self. More consequently of others and less of self.

This objective understanding of Christ as the principle of monastic sanctity, corporate and also personal, is abundantly evident in St Benedict's Rule. St Benedict makes the personality of Christ the key both to human relationships within the community and to the system of authority which governs the life.

In the Prologue to the Holy Rule the applicant to the religious life is addressed as one who will serve as a soldier of Jesus Christ. This is just the beginning: an appeal to the still untrained imagination with the thought of Christ the Leader.

The idea is given a more interior significance when St Benedict comes to speak of the position of the abbot in the community. He is now addressing monks; he calls for the exercise of faith. The abbot, he says, 'is considered to represent Christ'. In faith the monk must look for Christ in his abbot; in faith the abbot must recognize the responsibility of bearing Christ in himself.

The more ready a monk is to see Christ in authority, the more he is drawn into the life of faith. The more also he is drawn into the life of the community, which is the life of common obedience and common faith.

'The obedience which is given to superiors', says St Benedict, 'is given to God.' This is no new theory—our Lord voiced it when speaking to Pontius Pilate—but it is the foundation upon which the whole structure of the supernatural society rests.

Whether in His Church or in a monastery, God normally deals with man through men. Man has to apply to men in order to receive the sacraments, in order to learn about God, in order to fulfil his duties towards God's laws, in order to live as a functioning member of Christ's mystical body.

For the monk, even more precisely than for the Christian in the world, authority is vested with the supernatural. There is something more sacred about the person and position of the abbot than there is about the person and position of, say, a director of industry or a commander-in-chief.

The abbot's standing as *vices Christi in monasterio*[1] is thus a consequence of the Incarnation. God has become man; Christ has handed down His Father's authority through Himself to men; men, in their order, represent this authority to one another and transmit it to one another.

It is not power or dignity or even sanctity that is the link between Christ and the religious superior. It is Christ Himself that is the link. If the subject and superior alike do not see this in faith and act upon it, then on one side or the other there will be something essentially lacking. Neither power, dignity, nor sanctity can be authentic if it is not Christ's.

---

[1] Representative of Christ in the monastery.

Thus it is true to say that what the monk gives to his abbot in the way of respect, loyalty, obedience and so on, is the same in kind as what he gives to Christ. It is not the same in degree, but in kind. He is giving to the same Person, to the one Christ. The difference is only in the manner of his giving, mediated and refracted as it must be in the response which is made to the human representative.

Where authority is vested in a lesser official, in one chosen by the abbot to act as his representative, all the more faith is required. But here too, echoing down the line, the voice is to be heard in faith as the voice of Christ.

This fellow subject's mind may not be clear about the word of God which he has been deputed to interpret. He may even not be clear as to the terms of his authority or the meaning of his abbot. But because he is in a position to give orders, he is a fellow subject no longer but a superior. He stands to me as Christ.

Misinterpretation, clumsy and harsh delivery, indiscreet and even unwarrantable interpolations and additions: none of these things can make any difference to the message. And the message comes ultimately from God.

A chief of staff may despatch an order by a messenger who cannot read, who thinks that what he is carrying is a bundle of private letters or some sandwiches, who is a bad man in his private life, who is contemplating desertion or suicide or betrayal of his friends, but none of this makes any difference from the point of view of those to whom the despatch is addressed. Granted that the order reaches them, it is for them to carry it out.

'Thou hast placed men over our heads', quotes St Benedict from the forty-fifth psalm, and it is for us to set the head of Christ over theirs.

'There is far more virtue in submitting to one whose faults are evident' were the words of our Lord revealed to St Gertrude, 'than to one who appears perfect.' Because it costs us more? Partly on that account but not altogether. The real value of such submission lies in something more positive, more objective. We obey now because of faith and love, because of Christ.

Not only in those placed over him must the monk seek Christ, but in those who follow the same monastic life on his right and left. At the Divine Office, at meals, at recreation, the monk is surrounded by other Christs, *alteri Christi*. He is working with them or for them all day long.

To some types of mind, it comes more easily to see Christ in the exalted than in the humble, in the superior than in the equal. The principle is the same: the human soul is the dwelling-place of God, and faith is the light that shows it to be such. To be in command no less than to be commanded calls for faith, and if I am entrusted by God with subjects for whom I am responsible I must see them as representatives of Christ.

St Benedict insists that guests to the monastery be received with the reverence due to Christ, that the sick and the poor be treated in the terms of St Matthew's twenty-fifth chapter ('What you did to one of these My least brethren, you did to Me'), and that those who stray should be sought for in the name of Christ 'who had compassion on the infirmity of the one lost sheep of the flock'.

As the Holy Rule began with Christ, so it ends with Christ. 'Let monks in honour prevent one another, bearing patiently with one another's infirmities whether of body or mind. Let them vie with one another in their obedience. Let none follow what he thinks to be of profit to himself but rather that which is profitable to another. Let them show fraternal charity among themselves. Let them fear God, love their abbot with a sincere and humble affection, and *prefer nothing whatever to Christ*; and may He bring us to life everlasting. Amen.' From the Prologue to the Epilogue the dominant thought is Christ.

The Holy Rule is a curious document: it changes as you study it. What seems at first to be a coat of Jacob is seen at the end to be a coat without seam. What you take to be a code of enactments turns out to be a devotional, if not even a mystical, treatise. You come to see more and more that the whole thing circulates round Christ.

Following Him in renunciation, imitating Him in obedience, sharing His suffering by endurance and His love by fraternal charity, the monk comes to the perfection of his religious state. St Benedict knows no other spirituality than this.

3
COMMON PERFORMANCE

'JUST as the flower necessarily precedes the fruit', says St Bernard (preaching on the text from the Canticles, 'Stay me up with flowers, compass me about with apples'), 'so faith must of necessity go before good action.' The two preceding chapters have been mostly concerned with faith; the next two will be mostly concerned with good action.

'Since faith without works is dead', says St Bernard, quoting from St James, 'so it is useless for the flower to appear if it be not followed up by the fruit.'

Charity begins in the heart and head, but it must not end in the heart and head. Charity, like faith, is dead without works. For charity to be alive, there must be a real relation between the will to love and the works of love.

We have examined the common ideal of love; what now of the common practice?

As an introduction we can note the distinctions made by St Bernard in the virtue of charity. First there is the distinction between the charity that is directed by reason and the charity that is impelled by the fire of divine love. The one is dry but steady and strong; the other is full of unction. Then there is the distinction between affective and effective charity: the former is that of feeling, the latter that of action.

If the charity of feeling and the charity of action can be co-ordinated, the problem of community life has been solved.

The works of charity proceed from the combined activity of reason, desire, feeling. Of these, desire is the most important. But it is a reasoning desire, not an impulsive or an emotional desire. 'Let us be moved to the doing of good works rather by the powerful impulse of truth and fact than by a feeling of emotional charity.' St Bernard has no confidence in the stirrings of sentiment.

Affective charity, then, is the work of grace in the soul by which the obligations of love are set in their proper order. By affective charity the soul loves God before all things.

Effective charity, also of course the work of grace, goes out to meet the immediate necessity. By effective charity, the soul, loving God before all things, deals with the outward demands that are made upon its love and relates them to the final end of all, which is Love itself.

'Let us not love in word nor in tongue,' says St John, 'but in deed and in truth.'[1] This is effective charity, the practical outcome of the other.

But sometimes there is an apparent conflict between the charity of action and the charity of interior affection. What is the soul to do? Which need is to be followed? Here again St Bernard provides the answer.

'There is no doubt that in a right-thinking soul the love of God is preferred to the love of man, heaven to earth, eternity to time, the soul to the body. And yet in well-regulated action the opposite order is frequently, or almost always, found to prevail. For we are both more frequently occupied, and more busily, with cares for the temporal good of our neighbour, and among our brethren we assist with more diligence those who are infirm. We apply ourselves, by the right of humanity and the necessity of the case, more to promote the peace of the earth than the glory of heaven. In our anxiety about temporal interests we scarcely allow ourselves to think anything about those which are eternal … Who doubts that a man, when he is in prayer, is speaking with God? And yet how often are we withdrawn, and so

---

1 1 John 3:18

torn away from prayer—and at the very dictate of charity? ... How often does holy quiet give place, and that from a holy motive, to the tumult of business affairs? ... A preposterous order in which to act, but necessity knows no law.'

So, if we have St Bernard's authority for saying that effective charity, charity in act, is right to forget the relative value of things and remember the necessities of men, we have our justification for the demand, sometimes the excessive demand, of the common life. 'At least it is a charity kindly and just', says St Bernard. And with that he concludes the subject.

With the above as an introduction we can now examine the performance of monks living together in a monastery. The combined principles of fraternal charity and religious simplicity or humility will ensure two things: first, the smooth ordering of community intercourse; second, a standard of individual behaviour which is unextraordinary.

The obligation (as in marriage) is to respect, love, obey. It is not merely to avoid detesting the brethren. Nor do we begin by the avoidance of what is opposed to respect and love: we begin by trying to respect and love.

We also end by respect and love. The disagreements, even the quarrels, which occur in the course of living the common life are the differences which arise between friends. Disagreements which go deeper than this, or those which are kept up after the first flaring of annoyance, are of course ruinous to the religious life.

The kind of disagreement which leads to faction is ruinous not only to the religious life of individuals but also to the religious life of the community. The moment the monks start taking sides, the peace of the house goes.

If the thought of Roman fighting against Roman in civil war can sting the poet Horace into bitter comparison with the brute creation where animal attacks only animal of a different species, the thought of religious contending against religious should disturb us even more. Just as every act of charity builds up in the soul the likeness of Christ, so every act of uncharity blurs the image and weakens the hold of prayer.

The term common life should be synonymous with the term common charity: charity *is* the life of the community. If charity goes, the common life goes. Though the brethren may work, eat, sing at the Divine Office together, they are not, if they are out of charity, leading the common life.

The common life means putting in as well as taking out. It means contributing charity as well as benefiting by it. Religious charity is not the warm glow which we feel when our brethren show us kindness. Nor is it the warm glow which we feel when we show kindness to them. It is being actively charitable whether we happen to feel charitable or not.

Thus, the test of our common life is not in the abundance of our goodwill but in the effectiveness of our goodwill. The proof of the first *Gloria in excelsis* was shown in what happened next: the men of goodwill got up from their mountainside and went in search of Him who was promised. Finding Him, they found peace.

If we want to hear the voice of God telling us where to find our peace, we shall hear it in the summons to charity. Charity *is* our peace—our own and the community's alike.

We do not have to leave the community in order to find our peace; to find our true peace we have to sink ourselves in the community. We are tempted to feel that the company of the brethren at recreation and at work is a distraction, is noisy and unrestful and therefore something to be avoided. To feel this is to have a wrong idea of three things: true peace, the essential nature of distraction, and charity.

Perhaps our mistake lies in thinking of the common life as companionship. It may involve this, and there are times when a soul may have to rely upon the companionship of the common life, but companionship is only a sign and not the thing itself.

What satisfaction is to manual labour, companionship is to the common life. When we look for the outward sign and consequence more earnestly than we look for the thing itself we end up by missing both.

The common life is therefore a discipline before it is a consolation. To some it may be the most severe among the disciplines of the religious vocation. Certainly it is the most sanctifying.

Perhaps another mistake which we make is to think of common life in terms of security, whether personal or corporate. Here again there is a confusion between the expression and the thing expressed.

Security is to the common life what the sense of devotion is to prayer, or the sense of fittingness is to study and to the exercise of creative talent. In the spiritual life it is a mistake to put all your industry into producing a by-product.

The vow of stability, as we shall see in the concluding chapter, provides the element of security due to monastic life; but it is not the whole of security, either for the soul or for the community.

Both the soul and the community should find their true security in the Providence of God. How far the community manages to attain to this it is not for the individual member to judge. The individual soul's concern is to look for its spiritual security in nothing less than God.

Until the soul can rise to such a trust, the security afforded by the common life is a good deal safer to rest in than anything else. If a religious must have a temporal anchorage to give him the sense of confidence and peace, by all means let it be his community.

When God is rested in as the whole security, the soul will possess the true but relative security that the common life, better than any other, can provide.

But there can be neither companionship nor security where the essential quality of social intercourse, namely mutual confidence, is lacking. This does not mean that the brethren should be forever expressing their trust in one another. It means that they must believe in one another.

To believe in someone is to assume that his true norm is higher than what appears when he is acting normally. It is to expect that person to be capable of better than he thinks.

Ordinary occasions, such as come up in ordinary common life, are met by a more or less ordinary expenditure of effort. We see what is ordinary in each other's effort, and we tend to judge at this level. To have confidence in our brethren is to judge at the level of their possible effort, at the level of the extraordinary.

Want of confidence does not merely dismiss an opportunity, or even rule out a possibility; it puts up a barrier. Not to believe in someone actively prevents understanding. My lack of trust makes it impossible to see the person as a complete being. Equally it makes it impossible for him to see me.

Though loyalty may not absolutely depend upon mutual confidence—because you can be loyal to people whom you do not trust or understand—it is considerably helped by it. Loyalty in a community is the support which each member should be ready to offer to every other member and to the body as a whole. The community which could not command such loyalty, pride itself upon it, count upon it both in a crisis and on the flat, would be a very peculiar community. Certainly, for as long such uncertain fidelity prevailed, the essential life of the house would be in danger.

All the more of a threat to community life, consequently, is mutual suspicion. Nothing is so isolating, so productive of envy and bitterness. There can be neither peace of mind nor spiritual progress where the monk lets himself get tangled up in the thorny undergrowth of suspected motive.

Suspicion is nature's way of compensating for not having a legitimate grievance. The mind may not judge, perhaps has no evidence as material for judgment, so takes refuge in vague resentments which are no refuge. It is like scratching round a sore: there is no irritation in the area that is being scratched, but the action creates the appropriate illusion: the itch is really in the mind, though the fingers are pretending it is in the skin.

But it is not only in the silencing of prejudices, antipathies and inhibitions that the harmony of common life is preserved. It is in the cultivating of thoughtfulness, fellow feeling, and the virtues of family life in general.

The monk who has a true sense of common obligation and fraternal charity will go out of his way to be helpful; he will not hide when volunteers are called for; he will even foresee an occasion and offer himself for service.

To grudge time is to grudge charity. To resent interruption is to resent the echo and accent, if not the actual voice, of charity. It may also be to resent the same in regard to obedience.

If members of a natural family have to be accessible, members of a supernatural family have to be accessible to the point almost of invitation.

The supernatural family does not always have to take its lead from the natural family, but the resemblance between the two is close enough to make for salutary comparison. There are certain courtesies and customs, born of consideration for one another's feelings, which are observed in households in the world but often neglected in households of religion.

Common life should not mean uncouth life. The monk that is casual and ill-mannered, justifying his behaviour on the grounds that the religious life is above the ordinary conventions in use outside, has not learned from his spiritual life the delicacy of feeling which it should be teaching him.

To be scornful of expressions of gratitude and apology, never to show appreciation, to be ungracious in borrowing and lending: these are signs, not of unworldliness, but of insensitiveness.

Some may be more naturally considerate than others, but even the most thoughtless by nature should be able to avoid disturbing their brethren in a life where tranquillity is counted as both a means and a sign of progress.

The training is one partly of discipline and partly of grace. Certainly it should not require any extraordinary grace to make a man say his Mass in so quiet a voice as not to distract other priests saying Mass at other altars, to make a man forestall another's mistake in choir, to prevent him whispering little pleasantries in the *statio* or keeping up a mumbled commentary on the reading in the refectory, to give a man an eye for another's needs at work, at recreation, at meals, and when ill.

If a monk must renounce himself in order not to be a nuisance in the common life, he must also renounce himself in order not to be selective in the common life. The whole will not be balanced unless the parts are balanced, and the parts will not be balanced if preference is given to this or that at the expense of the common good.

In my work, in my relationships with others, in my recreations, in my devotions and private practices I must preserve an even pressure. A sense of proportion, increasingly informed by grace, should teach me the order to be observed. My own predilection, if indulged in, will play havoc with the order to be observed.

Once I allow my partiality for a particular employment, person, amusement, piety or custom to be the deciding voice in my decisions I am cutting myself off from the common life. In the case of the greater issues I should be able always to see the danger. Whether or not I shall avoid it is a different matter. But I shall find myself seeing more clearly and dealing more strongly if in the smaller issues I am careful to preserve detachment and balance.

Thus, there is a lack of unity in my service of the common good if I take trouble to prepare a sermon which will be heard by externs, but take no trouble to prepare a ceremony or the reading of some lessons which will affect only a few of my brethren. Again, I may go to great lengths to satisfy a guest while showing a dismissive attitude towards a fellow monk. I am ready enough to talk at length on my own subject when at recreation with the community, but am inclined to show boredom when other topics are discussed. I want a fixed time for my devotional exercises, and I do not like either charity or obedience or hospitality to interfere with what I have set myself to do for God in this way.

In all this there is a want of integrity and simplicity and truth. It means that I am being directed by a purely natural taste. The particular taste that upsets the harmony may lay claim to a supernatural colour, but in this context it is only another name for self-love.

The fancy that selects from the common stock, and works the selection as a private venture independently of the common need and practice, may pretend that it has God for its inspiration and end, but in fact it is just a fancy like any other. The religious life cannot be kept together by a string of fancies.

To conclude. In every religious community men of different temperament, age, upbringing, race and ability are set in one direction side by side. If their lives are to be presented to God in unity, they must accommodate themselves to each other's differences. In attempting to do this they must know that since they are associated together in Him, for Him, and by His will, they can rely infallibly upon the help of God's grace.

'Give me the man', says St Bernard in the peroration to one of the sermons from which we have already quoted, 'who before all things loves God with all his being, who loves both his neighbour and himself in the same degree in which each loves God, whose love for all other things is regulated by his love for God, who despises the earth and looks upward to heaven, who knows how to distinguish between those things which are to be chosen and loved and those that are to be merely used ... show me, I say, such a man as this, and I will boldly pronounce him wise, since he takes things for what they truly are and is able to boast with truth: He has set in order charity within me.'

Nothing calls for greater supernatural wisdom than the ordering of divine and human charity. If it were only the place of human charity in the scheme of divine charity that clamoured for definition, the problem would not be so hard to solve; but within that problem there is the other problem of how to order human charity. In the clarifying of this second issue, which is a lifetime's work, there is much scope for misconception.

4

COMMON MISCONCEPTIONS

IF solicitude for the needs of the brethren, coupled with discretion in balancing the duties of community life, were the whole of the matter, the secret of leading the common life might be learned in a year's novitiate. But it amounts to more than this. The harmony of community life further depends upon the disciplined reserve which forbids singularity.

Independence of judgment and action offends not only against humility but also against fraternal charity. Though this independence may spring from pride and self-love, purely personal qualities, the consequences of this independence account for a whole crop of sins relating to other people.

Assertiveness, ostentation, obstinacy, ruthlessness in getting one's own way: these are some of the manifestations. But these, after all, are matters for correction from the nursery upwards. What we are particularly considering here, in treating of the religious life, is singularity.

'The eighth degree of humility', says St Benedict, 'is when a monk does nothing except what is commanded by the common rule of the monastery or by the traditions of the seniors.'

A monk of spirit who takes his doubts on the score of monastic conduct to the bar of St Benedict's eighth degree of humility will know what course to follow. Self-effacement comes hard to the zealous, whether their zeal be true or false.

St Benedict sees in common behaviour the most immediate means to common charity. It is also common charity's most immediate expression.

Respect for the tradition of the seniors means respect for the seniors themselves. Respect for the common rule and custom leads to respect for those who observe the common rule and custom.

The idea of faithful conformity, to a pattern of conduct can be unfortunately presented. What it does not mean is rigid uniformity. What it does mean is united and harmonious activity.

In conforming to the traditions of his community a monk identifies himself with the mind of the place; he shows himself to be in active sympathy. Reverence for the traditions and customs is not the same thing as connivance at the abuses.

There is no degree of humility which obliges a monk to observe the common practice if it is a bad practice. But the monk must make sure that the practice in question is a bad and not an uncongenial one.

A monk seeks perfection according to a certain mode of life conditioned by a certain mode of interpretation. He takes what he has inherited from other monks as being the expression of God's will for him. If he co-operates, he is one in charity with his brethren and on the direct way to perfection. If he holds aloof, he is being singular.

A monk who is singular will find it almost impossible to reach perfection. He has cut himself off from the help of his brethren, he is guided only by his private judgment, he has no objective standards.

Besides offending against humility and charity, the monk who is singular offends against obedience, simplicity, and truth. It is highly likely that if he persists in his singularity he will offend also against his religious state.

How can a man be attentive to the needs of others when he is thinking only of his own? How can a man find it in him to be tolerant of the weaknesses of others when he judges their whole interpretation of life to be weak and wrong, and only his own to be strong and right?

The ideal held out by St Paul to the Philippians is the one to guide us if we are pledged to the pursuit of common perfection: 'Each one not considering the things that are his own but the things that are other men's.'[1]

In order to be *un*singular in community life, then, a man must be ready to learn both from history and from contemporary practice. He must be ready to assume that the experience of many is more likely to point to truth than the experience of one.

He must be ready to assume that the Holy Spirit is more likely to be found in balance than in over-emphasis. If his own particular leaning is against the common understanding of the point at issue, he must be ready to assume that this special emphasis of his is misconceived.

For a monk of pronounced monastic leanings, the assumption that his brethren are right and that he is wrong is an act of considerable faith and merit. If it were not, St Benedict would not have made a degree of humility out of it.

Singularity can express itself in countless different ways. Almost anything in the common observance can occasion it. Where the ordinary rules of mortifications fail to deal with it, singularity will be exorcized only by a radical change of outlook.

A man may get rid of his eccentricities by humbly following a system. He will not get rid of his independent ways of thought unless he substitutes other ways of thought. Once he has acquired the way of thought that is orthodox, he will find that his minor eccentricities will drop away. The whole being, man and mannerism, will be surrendered.

It is the thought that is the important factor. Once get the soul thinking humbly, charitably, unselfishly and in the single direction towards Christ, and you get the soul deciding and acting according to its state. The state under discussion is the monastic state.

There cannot be a division between the ethics of monasticism and the morality of monasticism. The conviction governs the conduct, the conduct justifies the conviction. The one may not be stressed at the expense of the other. Monastic orthodoxy must be verified in monastic orthopraxis: each feeds and supports the other.

By all means let a monk resolve to cure himself of wearing his vest-

---

[1] Philippians 2:4

ments or his habit differently from other people, of cultivating peculiarities in choir and in the refectory, of doing things at strange times or in strange places, of hurrying or moving too slowly, of attracting attention generally; but let him also, and more significantly, examine his primary monastic principles and see how far they are in line with the accepted view.

Have I a theory of my own about poverty, for example, or about hospitality, the care due to the sick, the recreation suitable for monks? Have I my own ideas about what kind of work should be undertaken, or not undertaken, by the community? Do I press my personal attraction with regard to the chant, to the architecture of the house, to the planning of the grounds? Am I wedded to particular penances, to particular studies, to manual labour, to my own horarium and to fads about food?

Unless I am prepared to detach myself from the excesses of what I am pleased to call my spiritual bent, I shall be at the mercy of individualism and impulse. My monastic prejudices can lead me past deviationism to social and spiritual isolation.

From holding that it is wrong for monks to smoke or drink wine, I shall come to absent myself from community recreations on the occasions when these things are allowed. From holding that it is right for monks to mount secular platforms I shall come to be seldom in my monastery. If I think that no monk may save his soul unless he reduces his meals to a minimum, I shall find myself becoming more and more fastidious in the refectory, less and less eager (or able) to take part in the common exercises of the community.

Natural and supernatural inclination must be measured against the accepted policy of the house. If the general feeling is opposed to my particular feeling I must think again before acting further.

Prayer is not the only light by which the cenobite is guided. Monks must allow themselves to be guided, indirectly and sometimes directly, by their brethren.

By the combined light of his own prayer and his brethren's experience, the monk should come to see in relief the relative values of religious principles.

By the combined force of his own prayer and mutual sympathy, the monk should be able to make the necessary sacrifices. In one instance he may find himself called upon to sacrifice a practice, in another his understanding of the principle behind it. The common life, no less than the prayer life, demands sacrifice.

Only when the soul has fully made its surrender to God in the will, and to the objective authority of superiors and community in the matter of practice, may what is believed to be the inspiration of grace be confidently followed up.

Nor may this belief be arrived at lightly. Nor may it go untested. Seriousness, purity of intention, trial over a period of time, advice and permission: all this will be needed by way of assurance before I can safely explore a course that is exceptional, that is singular.

Without such strict verification how should I dare to take risks? If I am to expose my singularity by going on missions of charity, by keeping up an enormous correspondence, by extending the ordinary practice of hospitality so that it involves extra disturbance or extra expense, by wearing myself out in a particular kind of work or a particular kind of penance, by resorting to exceptional methods in procuring for myself the solitude which seems to agree with my spirit, I must have very firm sanction indeed.

Having eliminated every mania in the cause of conformity, a man may now—such is the misapplication to which human nature is liable—make a mania of conformity.

Singularity is not only the exploiting of an idiosyncrasy; it is the carrying of an idea beyond its logical conclusion. A monk can sink himself so deeply in the common life as to fall through it and come out the other side.

To make a cult of anything is to exaggerate something.

If your whole effort is directed towards avoiding every fetish, you are creating a fetish.

You can cultivate moderation immoderately. Your desire for the norm can be abnormal, and you will find yourself practising humility out of pride and fraternal charity out of self-love.

If you confuse the ideal with the extreme, you go beyond the extreme into extravagance. Extravagance, in the religious vocabulary, is only another word for singularity.

The man who goes too far in any one direction is not able to see the scene as a whole. So of course, he makes these mistakes in proportion: his perspectives are all wrong.

Thus, the monk who shows his awakening to the ideal of common life by making community recreation the most important feature of monastic life is not in fact doing service to the common life. He has got hold of a good thing, but he is being singular about it.

Thus, if I so throw myself into the social life of the house as to extend the time and scope of regularized relaxation, and particularly if I do it on the rebound from following the ideal of solitude, I do harm to the common ideal.

By holding unnecessary conversations, by inviting my fellow monks to play cards when the game is not likely to be finished before the community is again in silence, by getting up community entertainments, by giving too much importance to the celebration of anniversaries, I am obscuring for others both the ideal which I have abandoned and the ideal to which I am now pledging myself. Also, I am probably being a great bore to my brethren.

In correcting an over-emphasis, I must avoid overemphasizing the correction. A reform loses much of its force if it requires another reform to restore the balance.

The fervour of a monk is not measured by his conspicuous observance but by his perfect observance. It is possible that the more fervent he is the less conspicuous his observance will be.

Where the community is a fervent one, the observance of individual members will not be conspicuous at all. Steam shows over warm water only when the surrounding temperature is cool. One light among many seems dazzling only when the others are not as bright.

The singularity which springs from fervour comes about under one of two conditions: either there is an excess of zeal in an individual or there is a deficiency of zeal in a community. The singularity which springs from tepidity comes of one condition only: the lack of religious spirit in the individual, whether in relation to his own or to the common ideal.

Religious are subject to other misconceptions besides those covered by singularity. These errors are all in the end found to arise out of independence of spirit. In itself there is nothing wrong in possessing an independent spirit—just as in itself there is nothing virtuous in possessing a submissive spirit—but when it leads to independence of policy and action it upsets the order of religious life.

High in the scale of additional misconceptions is the fallacy that health must come first. Certainly health is an important factor in the religious life, but quite as certainly it must not come first. Physical well-being, once allowed to get above its place in the scheme of religious values, is a tyrant.

From being a servant it can become the most exacting of masters. It can demand exemptions from the common life, interpret obedience and presume permissions, wound charity, override poverty, neglect penance and prayer, impose a rule of idleness and evasion.

Preoccupation about his health can gradually undermine not only a monk's observance but his whole religious attitude. He can become querulous, suspicious, grasping. He can come to view his brethren as existing for the purpose of ministering to his needs, come to treat his monastery as a nursing home.

Avoiding the choir, community recreation, the work of the place, a monk who makes his health an excuse for self-indulgence is more of a deviationist than the monk who makes the common life an excuse for self-indulgence.

To look for attention from sympathetic brethren is worse than to attract attention among unsympathetic brethren. Self-pity is more to be despised than self-advertisement.

The health-first fallacy gives rise to ancillary fallacies which in their degree affect the common life. Thus there is the fresh-air fallacy, which can be of considerable inconvenience to the community as well as being too much of a religion and a thing to be depended upon for the individual. There is the exercise fallacy, which again upsets the proportion of the monk's working day. And there is the diet fallacy, which is so obvious among fallacies as to need no comment.

Granted that his ill-health is perfectly genuine, a monk must have more serious grounds than a layman for retiring into the private life of the invalid. He must remember that, like Abraham, he has come out from his father's house and from among his kindred, and that whatever he might have expected from his family in the world he is living in a different family now. The ties which bind him to his brethren in religion are no less real than those which bound him to members of his family; but they are supernatural instead of natural, and they suppose a different scale of obligation.

'I have left my house, I have renounced my inheritance'—to quote again the *Introit* of St Benedict Joseph Labre's Mass—'but the Lord has taken hold of me.'

The monk is not likely to want for medical attention in his monastery, still less for the support and attention of his brethren, but he should know that where laymen have the right, if they can afford them, to luxury and expensive treatment in their illnesses, religious have no such claim to the comforts of the world.

The monk who expects to be treated with greater consideration because he is a monk is growing smaller as the result of his sickness. Both as a monk and a man he is shrinking in character. Ill-health is meant to make people nobler, not meaner.

It would be a sad commentary on the religious life if monks and nuns were found to make worse patients than men and women in the world. Yet it is only too possible for religious to take advantage of being delicate. It seems that neither the habit nor the vows can prevent us from being inconsiderate, demanding, envious, impatient and immortified. Still more strange that having pledged ourselves to religious poverty we can indent for cures and convalescence regardless of expense.

Such failure to respond to the summons of ill-health must argue a want of supernatural faith. If we really believed that our disabilities were signs of God's love, were intended for our sanctification, were dependent for remedy upon His Providence, we would not rely so much on medical aid and human commiseration.

The religious should be the first to see sickness in terms of the supernatural. To him it should be a God-given opportunity, a grace. As a challenge to generosity there can be few things so stimulating as a good illness.

But so often it evokes nothing but self-pity and a craving for the good things that the vows have renounced. If ill-health led only to a solitude in which the soul might develop at leisure the life of prayer and reading, it would do no harm to the sufferer's community spirit and would bring down graces upon the community as a whole. But sometimes it leads to a bitter isolation, and the cultivation of a taste for sybaritic ease.

If there is error in attaching too much importance to health, there is a parallel error in attaching too much importance to money. The note struck here is more impersonal than in the other case—because the individual religious is not wanting money for himself—but perhaps on that account the evil is all the more insidious.

Buoyed up by a sense of altruism the monk sets himself to make all the money he can, and then lays his gains at the feet of his abbot and community. Imagining himself to be entirely selfless, he is in effect taking a highly singular line.

The monk who thinks that he has satisfied his obligation towards his brethren when he has made money for them is missing the significance of community life. With the best intentions he is committing a form of simony: he is buying something holy.

Beyond its mercenary implications, such an attitude towards common work and common life is an affront to humility as well as to poverty and charity. It is virtually saying, 'All you have to do is to come to me.'

To hoard possessions or money is blatantly wrong; but it is also wrong to hoard prestige. To adopt a patronizing attitude towards those of humbler origins than oneself is blatantly against the religious spirit; it is also against the religious spirit to show condescension to those who are not bringing in as much as oneself to the common funds.

No one member of a community is in a position to confer favours upon his brethren. On this subject St Benedict could not be more clear: 'If there be artificers in the monastery, let them exercise their craft with all humility, provided the abbot shall have ordered them. But if any of them be proud of the skill he has in his craft, because he thereby seems to gain something for the monastery, let him be removed from it.'

It is possible for religious, following the same line of error, to canonize a false community pride. They can come to see something holy in the prestige and wide material influence of their house. If for all religious who live in communities this is a possible misconception, it is especially so of those who take a vow of stability and who consequently owe special obligations of loyalty to the monastery of their profession.

Good name and religious influence are things to be prized: they are held in common, and as coming from God. It is not the same where it is a question of fame and public favour: to rejoice in the monastery's high standing in the eyes of the world is a form of vanity like any other.

The only pride which is worth having in a community is that of charity: common supernatural gratitude for supernatural grace corporately enjoyed. This is holy, the other is not. And if you like to call it pride, you may.

To see the community's prosperity, or the lack of it, with the financier's eye (or the farmer's, estate agent's, prospector's, builder's or politician's) instead of with the eye of faith is to see it incompletely: is indeed to see it quite wrongly. It is also to court a whole host of further misreadings.

The phrase that is so often heard from religious, 'It would save money' to do this or that, is not always such a proclamation of holy poverty as it sounds. Religious poverty was not invented to save money.

Nor is the companion phrase, 'It would prevent so much waste', necessarily the bugle call of poverty. Holy poverty is for other things besides preventing waste. Holy poverty is designed, on the negative side, as a means of renouncing the natural acquisitiveness of man, and on the positive side as a means of following Christ and giving glory to God.

At the root of the matter is, again, the conflict between the natural and the supernatural. As in the question of health so in that of money and influence: the whole thing depends upon the degree of truth with which it is said 'I trust in God'.

If the two remaining mistaken approaches to the common life are dealt with briefly it is not because they are unimportant but because they are mistaken approaches to other forms of life besides the cenobitic. Religious misconceptions certainly, but not specifically monastic.

The first consists in believing that one's effort is wasted in the work given one to do; the second in resorting to every sort of unnecessary stimulus so as to avoid this waste. Both again spring equally from lack of faith.

The first takes the form: 'I would do much better in other occupations; I am unsuited; I have never had my chance; I know myself well enough to see that this work is the worst thing for me; they do not understand me here; I am a misfit, a failure; I give up.'

In such a state of mind there are to be found a variety of failings: vanity, discouragement, ambition, envy, resentment, restlessness and self-pity. The implication is that while one is capable of reaching the heights, one is, in fact, and on account of mismanagement somewhere, chained down in the valleys. Clearly there is in all this no recognition of God's design.

The self-distrust that does not lead to confidence in God, leads away from God and towards disgust, defeat, and hopelessness. When the setting of this sense of lost opportunity is a religious community, the repercussions are more serious than they would be if the setting were in the world.

But the man in religion has less excuse for sinking into this delusion than the man in the world. Religious life has the life of faith as its theme. The monk should know, if anyone should, that there is here no waste of effort, of talent.

If there has been mismanagement, it has been within the soul itself: it has been where the soul has failed to adjust itself to the apparent mismanagement of its outward affairs.

However incongruous the outward disposition of affairs, the monk is safe in judging that a congruity exists before God. And this is all that matters. His obedience ensures the supernatural character of the situation with which he is faced.

'If hard or impossible commands be enjoined a brother', says St

Benedict towards the end of his Rule, 'let him receive them in all simplicity and obedience. If he sees that the burden is altogether beyond his strength, let him patiently and in due order state the cause of his incapacity to his superior without show of pride, resistance, or contradiction. If after his suggestion the superior shall persist in his command, let the brother know that it is for his good, and trusting in the assistance of God let him obey through the love of Him.'

So it is the greatest delusion for a monk to imagine that his work in the house is unfortunately chosen or is not allowed for in the plan of Providence. It is lack of faith that sees accidents everywhere in the religious life.

The last of the self-deceptions to be mentioned here (and the one which we have linked with the one immediately above) is that which makes culture and current affairs indispensable to spiritual alertness. It might be called the sophistication fallacy.

'If my advice is sought by souls in their difficulties, and if my prayer is to be at all related to the intellect'—this is the argument—'I must keep my mind stirred and active. It is therefore my duty to stimulate its life with matters of educative and contemporary interest.'

There is something in this—just as there is something in the theory about fresh air and the spiritual life—but not much. The test of the theory will lie at the point where necessary stimulus ends and unnecessary interest begins.

Certainly some sort of study is needed, as we have already seen, if there is to be a fruitful spiritual life. But it is not so much a question here of study as of curiosity. Intellectual curiosity, in the frame of the religious life, is no better than any other appetite. In fact, being generally held to be superior, it can be more damaging than most. It comes in disguised. It carries a spurious refinement and nobility.

A monk may persuade himself that in filling his mind with ideas and images from secular literature he is realizing a laudable purpose. Accordingly, he will set out to be well informed on every worldly subject, will strive to keep abreast of every movement, political and religious, as presented by the press of every shade of opinion, will want to read the most recent book and hear the most authentic broadcast.

'Otherwise', says the monk in his humility, 'I find myself becoming just a cabbage.'

If the soil is the religious life, it is perhaps better to be the lowly vegetable than a forced fruit or hot-house flower.

As part of the defence-mechanism a man will screen his natural curiosity behind a sheaf of religious periodicals. At least this is better than using the bookstalls of the world. While not going so far as the rector of great sanctity who used to tell his seminary students on the eve of their departure for the ministry, '*Ne lisez jamais es petits journaux religieux*'[2] we might profitably reduce our incidental reading, ecclesiastical as well as lay, to the minimum. It would leave us more time for the solid stuff of the Fathers. And the accredited spiritual writers of the Church.

Sophistication is not a snare to the truly sophisticated. To the religious, who is dedicated to the culture of the love of God, it may be.

Deliberately to entertain delusions such as have been discussed above is not only to prejudice both the ordered life of the religious family and the operation of grace in the individual soul, but is also to injure the faculties themselves which are called into play.

By viewing life too humanly, the soul's humanity—apart altogether from its spirituality—loses something of what is due to its completeness. It diminishes in sensibility. By taking a too materialistic stand, the material itself is handicapped.

If I fill my mind with the niceties of literature when I should be filling it with the mysteries of God, I take the edge off my critical faculty. My appreciations, because diverted from their proper object, are blunted. The proper object of the soul set towards God in religion is God Himself. If I use nail-scissors for cutting out Christmas decorations I spoil the blades. And so, over the whole list of mistaken apprehensions.

The only sure practice in all these things is to look for the supernatural substance in every issue and to make up for that. The natural accidents are the enemy to the supernatural good.

---

[2] Never read small religious newspapers.

If I fail to follow this course, my imagination—aided by a cabal consisting of emotions, inherited allergies, casts of training and twists of personal influence—will drag me down to the terrestrial and keep me there.

'But to him that overcometh', is the promise of the Apocalypse. 'I will give the hidden manna, and will give him a white counter, and in the counter a new name written which no man knoweth but he that receiveth it.' God will communicate these mysteries to the soul that has learned its lesson of perfect charity. Then will all shadow of misconception be swept away, and in the common life shared by the blessed in heaven the soul will know at last what it is to love.

5

COMMON PROGRESS

THE conclusion might be drawn from what has been said in the two preceding chapters that progress in the conventual life is progress in simplicity. The deduction would not be far wrong.

Almost all problems connected with either the interior and personal religious life or the exterior and common life can be solved by simplicity. But there is this condition: it has to be the simplicity that is of God.

Spiritual and religious simplicity is called in the Scriptures 'meekness'. '*Docebit mites vias suas*',[1] we have in the psalms, and our Lord tells us to learn of Him because He is 'meek and humble of heart'. 'Blessed are the meek', He says again, 'for they shall possess the land.'

Simplicity or meekness means this: trusting in God and not in anything less than God, rejecting the temptation to introspection and multiplicity, freeing oneself from motives and pretensions which lead to the many forms of exhibitionism.

Thus the religious who looks to God in his undertakings, who does not care whether people think him clever or stupid, strong or weak, successful or a failure, who takes it for granted that if God wants him to make any change in his life the grace will be there to show what the

---

1 He shall teach the meek His ways.

required change is and to provide the strength to make it, is showing himself to be simple and is making rapid progress in perfection.

The first condition for perfection is confidence in the power of God to perfect: not only in the power, but in the desire of God to perfect.

The last obstacle to perfection is disquiet about the possibility of being perfect. Only the simplicity of faith can stifle the disquiets of the spiritual life.

Only the simplicity of faith can at the same time rid the soul of its faulty preconceptions and draw it along towards the simplicity of God. Progress is the finding of this affinity. The soul joins God in a union of simplicity.

Until the final consummation, the soul is all the time simplifying, unifying, growing in purity and likeness. Likeness to God means likeness to Christ, and therefore likeness to Christ's love for men.

Thus, simplicity and charity go together. In this simplicity are contained faith, truth, humility; in this charity are contained all the virtues. Progress in the common life, then, and progress in the interior life are one thing.

Growth in Christ means growth in His mystical body, growth in fraternal charity. All this is as easy to recognize as it is difficult to practise. How shall we ever begin to do what we are told?

Every time we take part in a community exercise we are being drawn, whether we notice it or not, into closer union with Christ's mystical body. We are advancing in love. We are advancing literally in *His* love; ours we know very little about and dare not measure.

Our progress is His love; His love is our progress. It is as if in a strange land we asked someone for a stamp, and looked up to find, that the person's face was the same as that on the stamp. It is as if we were buying a statue, and were borrowing the money from the person who owned it, who had been the model for it, and who actually *was* it.

In all that we want it is really Christ. In all that we find it is really Christ. Our very wanting and finding is Christ. We have nothing that we have not borrowed, we make no progress that is not His.

The three ideas, which are only three aspects of the same idea, are reflected in the words of the bride to the Bridegroom: 'Draw me after Thee; we will run in the fragrance of Thy ointments.' 'Draw me', for

I cannot move a step without Thee: 'No man can come to Me unless the Father who has sent Me draw him.' Next 'we will run and our progress will be hastened by the unction of the Spirit and not by our own enthusiasm and sense of competition. Thirdly 'we will run'—together, in the plural, as a body.

Not to spoil the work of being 'drawn after Thee' we need the grace of simplicity. We must believe that when our Lord said, 'Without Me you can do nothing', He meant exactly that. *With* His help we can lead His life. Our tragedy is that even with His help we sometimes refuse to.

St Bernard says that though all men desire to obtain happiness from Him, few desire to follow Christ. Few desire to be drawn along the whole way. 'Even carnal men want for themselves the death of those who are spiritual', he says, 'yet shudder at the idea of leading their life.'

To 'run after Thee' without hindrance comes only when the soul follows in spirit and in truth. That is to say in simplicity. 'I have run in the way of Thy commandments,' says the psalmist, 'since Thou hast set my heart at liberty.'

Great liberty is granted to the soul that is determined to run, come what may, at the drawing of Christ. Such a soul runs in good company. If Seneca preached the doctrine that a man possesses within himself a power which is beyond defeat, and that it is the duty of men to keep alive the conviction that no outside power can reduce the soul to captivity, it is the doctrine of St Paul that 'in all these things we overcome because of him that has loved us'. The potentialities of human nature are brought to Christian actuality by grace, by love.

'I am sure', St Paul goes on in his Epistle to the Romans, 'that neither death, nor life, nor angels, nor principalities, nor powers, nor things present, nor things to come, nor might, nor height, nor depth, nor any other creature shall be able to separate us from the love of God which is in Christ Jesus our Lord.' Here is Seneca's liberty made spiritual; here are simplicity and faith. To come more and more to believe this and to live by it is to advance.

Spirituality is progressive, is in constant movement. Though the Holy Spirit sets the pace of the advance, the soul must know that there can be no delaying on the way. The soul must hear the word of God and keep up with it. '*Qui emittit eloquium suum terrae; velociter currit sermo ejus.*'[2] There is to be running in this. 'It were better for me that Thou shouldst keep me close to Thee', says St Bernard, 'even by the use of a measure of violence, by making me afraid with Thy threatenings or causing me to smart with punishments, than that Thou shouldst spare me in my evil and slothful security, and leave me to myself. Draw me after Thee, even it be in some sort against my will that Thou mayest make me willing.'

Twice in the Holy Rule, once at the beginning and once at the end, St Benedict speaks of 'hastening' in the way of God's commandments. The growth of faith combined with the enlargement of the heart will see to it, he tells us, that the course is run with 'unspeakable sweetness and love'.

We run lonely but not alone. In this kind of race our fellow competitors are not rivals but fellow lovers. We are anointed with the same unction and fed from the same 'storerooms of the King'. By mutual example and exhortation, the followers of the Bridegroom verify outwardly the action of the Holy Spirit within.

As the soul draws near to the Beloved, the just will ask in the words of the Canticle, 'Who is this that cometh up from the desert, flowing with delights?' and the Beloved, recalling the soul's redemption in the shadow of the cross, will say, 'Under the apple-tree I raised thee up'. Then will the soul know beyond all doubt that its raising up, its progress in the spiritual life, has been no work of its own but wholly by the grace of the Beloved.

'So then', in St Paul's conclusion, almost as if he were setting himself to comment on the Canticle, 'it is not of him that willeth, nor of him that runneth, but of God that showeth mercy.'

It is a mark of the soul's advance in the spiritual life when interior conflicts and exterior pressures are alike endured without fuss. This does not mean that these things are endured with sweetness, but that the bitterness which they cause is accepted, blindly, along with the rest.

---

2   Who sendeth out his speech to the earth; his word runneth quickly.

The soul, reduced to nothing, makes acts of faith and humility, and looks no further into its reactions to the particular trial of the moment. The fact that these acts of faith and humility feel empty of meaning makes no difference. The soul, quite rightly, goes on making them.

The trials to which the advanced are subject may or may not be more severe than those which test the less advanced. Trials, anyway, are relative. The point here is that the advanced are less disturbed by them.

The advanced will feel their sufferings more, but they will meet them with less agitation. Those who are not so advanced will suffer their trials, whether objectively greater or smaller, with less pain but with more upset. By upset we mean self-pity, discouragement, failure in hope and trust.

Take the common case of the religious who wants to serve God in full perfection but who is oppressed by petty obligations. He feels that his fruitfulness as a servant of God and his happiness as a human being depend upon a measure of solitude, upon leisure for prayer and spiritual reading.

When such a man finds himself engaged for a large part of the day in what appear to be useless interviews, finds himself smothered by a correspondence to which he cannot give proper attention, finds himself called upon to produce work which he knows will suffer from want of preparation, what does he do? Either he reserves to himself the right to feel bitter about it and to keep up a rearguard defence against it, or, refusing to examine his emotional response, he yields and takes it calmly.

Where one man may struggle with his problem in a mood of such distaste and tension that every telephone call will be an occasion of revolt, another will submit in faith to the plan as a whole.

Where one man may try to find some sort of mental refuge to which he can escape while his body is present to deal with interruption after interruption, another will address himself to the actuality and accept it as part of his vocation.

Where one man can look forward only to seeing an end of his labours, another looks forward only to seeing God more clearly in his labours.

It is not that the man who is further advanced is less naturally antipathetic to his lot in life—he may hate it just as much as the other, and will probably, as we have seen, feel some of its aspects more—but that he is more supernaturally in tune with it.

The desire to escape may be intense in each man, but where the more advanced treats it as a daydream to be dismissed like any other, the less advanced treats it as a passion which he has to fight every inch of the way.

The longing for death, again, which may be as ardent and constant in the life of the advanced soul as it is in that of the less advanced takes a different form in each. To the one who is imperfect, who is opposing the inescapable, it presents the idea of release and can become an obsession. To the one who faces the realities of his life and believes that God will make them bearable, the thought of death is not so much an escape as one more aspect of hope.

It is not necessarily an obstacle to its progress that a soul should yearn, and yearn almost to desperation, for death. The question turns on the manner of its yearning, and what difference it makes in the conduct of inward and outward affairs. To clarify this issue a long quotation from De Osuna's *Third Spiritual Alphabet* will serve.

'Proficients should desire to be dissolved,' says this authority, 'that the kingdom of heaven may come so that they may behold the King in His beauty with which love is satisfied. To ascertain that this desire comes from genuine love, it must be found so firmly fixed in the soul that neither human reason, nor delay, nor effort, nor fear, nor anything else in the world can effect it; for after we have given a thousand reasons to one who holds it to prove that it is not well to wish to die, he answers in his heart, not by words, but by a true interior act by crying to God : "O my Lord, take me to Thee." If we tell him that the vessel often longs to reach the port in order to escape the tempests and that sometimes it founders and goes to pieces, and that in the same way some persons think that they will be able so to escape the storms of this life and safely reach the port of heaven but founder on the rocks instead, he who so loves God that he wishes to die will reply, "It is impossible for a man to save himself by his own strength, but God supplies the needs" ... I tell you this in order that, if you should feel a sincere desire to die and go to God, you may not suppose it comes from yourself ... because it is combined with a trustfulness that makes it impossible for the soul to doubt that the Lord will show it mercy. The third love, that of the perfect, calms this longing, and enables them to bear life patiently. They make the third petition: "Be Thy will done in me on earth as it would he were I in heaven, for whether I die or whether I live, I am Thine. If I were to die it would only be to go to Thee; since I live, may I live for Thee?" Such have no will of their own; it is grafted in that of God.'

To confirm and conclude this matter of wanting to die we have the prayer of St Bernard himself: 'O lengthy little while! Good Lord, dost Thou call that a little while in which we do not see Thee? With all good respect to Thy word, my Lord, I must confess that it is long to me; yes, much too long. Yet it is right to call that time both short and long. For it is short compared with our deserts and very long indeed compared with our desires.'

In the practical field, and to the souls concerned, the distinction between the two attitudes becomes abundantly clear. It is simply the distinction between the right and the wrong way of meeting the cross.

The advanced soul rules out—anyway in the will—the bittersweet solace of resentment, self-pity, evasion. The imperfect soul leaves room for these things, and is therefore at the mercy of circumstance. Circumstances weigh heaviest on the weakest part, the part that is most exposed to danger.

Once we allow our sensitive nature to complain of the pressure of circumstances, we are vulnerable, not only in the part most exposed, namely the feelings, but also in the will. Transitory things can be wounding to the essential nature of man. We can allow outward events—even the pace of outward events or the idea of outward events—to become too much for us. We cannot keep up, so we let go altogether and subside into despair.

Instead of brooding over the things which we dread, we should look for supernatural peace *in* the things which we dread. Instead of seeing in every happening a new nightmare to be overcome by grace and determination, we should see in every nightmare a new manifestation of grace.

We are not asked to overcome our sufferings but to undergo them. It is not determination that will help us here, but surrender: surrender, through circumstances, to God.

If we meet every horror with clenched teeth we add to the tension in the will, and though there may be a suggestion of heroism about this there is nothing holy in strain as such. Indeed, there is far more holiness in the opposite, in serenity.

If on the other hand we acquire the habit of judging from God's angle, of allowing His eternal values to become ours, we grow to be almost proof against strain. Where there is nervous tension, there can be no true disposition for prayer.

Yet there are souls who feel that they must produce a nervous breakdown to prove the heroism with which they have been bearing their crosses. 'Every summons from the cell deprives me of the recollection which is vital to my spirit; every postal delivery does me violence; the element to which I have a right is forever being disturbed; I am being driven mad.'

All such maladjustment in spirituality is the result of not having faith, of not being humble. There would be none of this trouble if we believed that God could make us holy in His way more quickly than we can make ourselves holy in our own.

Holiness is not a matter of having time to pray; having time to read, prepare our work, follow up our work, give advice. Holiness is not a matter of time at all, or a matter of place. It is a matter of finding God's will in whatever is going on at the time, and wherever it is going on.

If we believe that God can use other means besides ourselves to convey His messages to souls, why do we worry when He deprives us of the leisure to prepare the delivery of His word? Why do we worry about not being able to catch up on our letters when we should know that He can answer our correspondents' questions better than we can? Why do we worry about not getting enough prayer for ourselves when we should know that whenever He removes one means of imparting Himself to the soul He provides another?

Faith and humility would between them resolve most of these difficulties. There are further difficulties which, because they are more interior, require an even greater measure of faith and humility. The conflicts which we have been examining are occasioned by outward contingencies. There are conflicts also which have nothing but what is inward to act as provocation. And these last are by far the most severe.

If the soul's advance is gauged by the way in which it handles its trials, detaches itself from natural perceptions, searches after the love of God before all else, then the more interior the activity, the less perceptible will be the progress. The ordinary signs and standards will, at that level, fail to register.

But the same law applies: there is the same need for faith and humility. In its desolations, obscurities, doubts, the soul must be guided as it was before—by the rule of surrender and trust. The same sanctions must be imposed: no self-pity or escape. For the rest it is a matter simply of perseverance. The refusal to be disturbed is now the one and only test.

'But that', you will object, 'is precisely the difficulty. If I could stay serene, I would know that all was well. But I cannot stay serene for two days together. I am as changeable as the April sky, altering with every fleeting mood. Elated one minute, plunged in wretchedness the next; hungering for every kind of worldliness one minute and for the fuller service of God the next; keyed up to confidence one minute and flattened by despair the next. I know that if I could become settled in the service of God it would be all right, and I would have peace. I know that if I were settled in worldliness, it would be all wrong, but again I feel I would have peace. But I feel I do not belong anywhere; I feel I have no place. One cannot be serene without a place. There is no misery like that of being rootless.'

This sense of homelessness and insecurity is superficial. Variation in mood is only variation in mood—not in will or in direction. Where the essential part of the soul is rooted and founded in charity, the surface disturbances are nothing to worry about. It is the surface disturbances that keep the soul aware of its helplessness, aware of its dependence upon God alone.

That all this pendulum-swinging is allowed for in the scheme of grace is shown by St Bernard where he speaks to his monks about the same kind of alternations. 'He who walks in the spirit does not remain always in the one state nor make progress always, with the same ease; because the way of man, as the Scripture says, is not in his own power… do not ever say in your abundance "I shall never be moved" for fear lest you should also be obliged to make use with grief of the words which follow: "Thou didst hide Thy face and I was troubled" … you will retain among the changeableness of earthly conditions, which are at one time prosperous and at another time adverse, as it were an image of eternity. I mean to say that you will maintain this equableness of spirit and a constancy not to be shaken by any event.'

Progress must be even progress, not to be shaken by any event. Yes, but how can I *not* be shaken by events? It is not as though I *liked* being shaken. What can I rest on that is firm inside myself, how can I convince myself that I have foundations that I cannot see and a serenity that I cannot feel?

Again St Bernard: 'You will at all times bless God'—this is the proof of it—'and will thus make good for yourself a position of immovable stability among the changing events and inevitable disappointments of this inconstant world, until you shall begin to be renewed and to take upon you once more the likeness of God who is eternal, "with whom there is no change nor shadow of alteration."'

Here you have the serenity which is not of natural poise but of supernatural faith; not of sentiment but of spirit. As the wall remains the same however many shadows pass across it, and as the looking glass remains the same however many changes of expression it reflects, so the soul that is held fast in God remains uninfluenced by the waving shapes and images that come and go.

True inward serenity will show itself, not perhaps to the soul but certainly to others, in a hundred small outward ways. There will be a certain reserve about the soul who is advancing in the spiritual life, a certain control and economy of speech, movement, gesture, which was not so noticeable before. Reverence, custody of the eyes, absence of flurry and haste will be practised instinctively: the outward will manifest the order that obtains within.

The effect upon others, though on the soul's part there is not the smallest desire to edify or attract attention, is considerable. By his outward conduct the man of God, as St Francis and others have taught, silently preaches the word of God. But recollected behaviour bears witness, after all, only to what the grace of God has done in the case of an individual soul. The indirect influence of a soul advancing in God's love is far greater.

Even if there were no outward signs to act as evidence, the mere fact of increasing holiness is an influence, is communicative. The soul that has entrusted itself wholly to the care of God and who is trying to walk in His ways has a power for good that is incalculable.

'He that believeth in Me, out of his bosom, as the Scripture saith, shall flow rivers of living water.' The soul of faith is an aqueduct, a channel of grace. The soul that is not advancing in the life of faith is not the influence on others that he might be.

A community of souls, each one made over to the unqualified way of grace, is a citadel of God, a stronghold impervious to attack. Its progress in true spirituality is manifested in its policy, in its customs, in its conduct. You feel, when you visit such a house, that its essential element is the element of prayer. You get the impression that the individual religious, as they move about, have a sense of direction. They appear neither rushed nor listless nor tensely purposeful, but at home in their Father's house with the work which is His to fulfil.

If according to Ecclesiasticus 'it is better that two should be together than one, for they have the advantage of their society', a body of religious men living together in charity have the greatest advantage of all: they can help one another to move forward in the one work that supremely matters.

The sum of all that has been said in this chapter, indeed in this book, is given in the twenty-fifth stanza of St John of the Cross's Spiritual Canticle:

> In Thy footsteps
> The young ones run Thy way;
> At the touch of the fire,
> And by the spiced wine,
> The divine balsam flows.

There is no advance but in the footsteps of the Beloved, and at the touch of the divine fire the humblest beginner is enabled to run. Stimulated by the spiced wine of fraternal charity, and shining with the oil of the love of God, the soul comes quickly to realize its vocation in Christ. 'Caritas Dei diffusa est in cordibus nostris per inhabitantem Spiritum ejus in nobis.'[3]

---

3   The charity of God is spread abroad in our hearts through the indwelling of the Holy Spirit in us—cf. Romans 5:5.

6
COMMON PERFECTION

IF common progress depends upon individual progress, not only will common perfection depend upon individual perfection, but the kind of perfection will correspond.

Thus, the common perfection of a house of friars will differ from that of a house of monks. The common perfection of a nursing or a teaching congregation will differ from that of either friars or monks.

It is not a question of which is more perfect—that of the friars, the monks, the religious of a society or congregation—but of how to realize in community the specific perfection proposed.

Nor is it a question of which is more social—the common life of the friary, monastery, or community house—but of how to develop in unison the social sense peculiar to the spirit of the order.

Much of what follows may, and it is hoped will, be of use to religious of whatever order. Those chiefly to be considered here, however, are the religious who bind themselves to a particular community as much as to a particular rule or order.

When we talk of the 'sons of St Benedict' we are thinking of all who follow the Holy Rule; when we talk of the 'Benedictine family' we think of a community.

The family of St Francis or of St Dominic is understood in a different sense: it does not refer to the priory but to the order. In becoming a Benedictine, a man joins a monastery, and will belong to that monastery. In becoming a religious of the non-monastic orders, a man joins the institute, and will belong to that institute before he belongs to any one religious house.

Thus, to the monastic orders, canons regular, certain orders of enclosed nuns, the meaning of family life is not the same as it is to other institutes. And because the idea is different, the obligation and practice will also be different.

The member of a community which is of fixed personnel has an outlook on the religious life which is quite different from that of the man who lives among brethren who might equally well be in any other house of the province.

Where the monk is expected to strike roots in the place which he enters, other kinds of religious are expected not to. Where the monk undertakes to stay where he is for the rest of his life, other kinds of religious undertake to exchange their communities at the shortest notice if this is the will of their superiors.

Where the monk is encouraged to look forward to years of sameness, to find his joy as well as his cross in the routine work of the house, the religious of another order is encouraged to widen his horizons and to train himself in the various different works which he may be summoned to perform.

The one kind of life calls for constancy and the willingness to sink oneself in the accepted environment; the other for detachment and flexibility. The one leaves no loophole open for a change from house to house; the other pulls no strings to secure a fixed place in any house.

Again, it is not a question of which is the more perfect, whether to hand oneself over to a permanent family or to hand oneself over to being transferred from family to family, but of how to perfect the particular vocation and so contribute to the perfection of the whole.

'St Benedict wished his disciples to be holy', writes Abbot Tosti in his biography of the saint and founder, 'but to the perfection of the individual he wanted to unite the social perfection of the cenobitical family.'

Social perfection in the Benedictine understanding of the term means that the monks, striving individually after charity in the full and twofold sense, hold their prayer, work, interests, duties, penances and pleasures permanently in common.

The cenobitical life is the religious family life conducted in a rather special way and based upon rather special foundations. How far this differs from any other form of conventual life will be seen if the principles of Benedictine conventual life are examined.

The more characteristic features of Benedictinism owe their origin to two things: the vow of stability and the position of the abbot in the community. Stability insures the same kind of relationship that exists between brother and brother in a natural family; the abbot rules the monks as a father rules his children.

A natural family in which the children come and go may still be a family, but it is much more of a family if everyone in it is living at home. Nor can parents exchange their children for others.

A natural family which is abandoned by the father may still be a family, but it is much more of a family if the father remains head of the household. Nor can one father be exchanged for another.

To live in one's monastic family according to the Benedictine view is to see the monastery, not as a domicile, but as a household, a home. It is to see one's brethren as one sees one's own brothers: depending upon them, being depended upon by them. It is to view one's abbot in a closer and more permanent relation to oneself than that implied in the idea of superior.

Stability sees to it that the brethren are more than fellow residents. The office of abbot sees to it that they are more than fellow subjects.

The monk who thinks of his community as an aggregation of men and not as a family unit is missing the specifically monastic character of the life. He may be following the conventual life, but he is hardly following the cenobitical ideal.

The monk who thinks of his abbot as a judge, an instructor, a master, is missing the specifically monastic character of authority. He may be fulfilling his vow of obedience, but he is hardly responding to the idea of sonship.

Nor is this developed conception of conventual life an incidental interpretation of the Holy Rule; it is part of St Benedict's original plan. It is not an unforeseen consequence of a particular legislation; it is the designed effect of a legislation drawn up with just such a purpose in view.

St Benedict introduced stability into existing monasticism, not as a preventative measure, but as a unifying measure. His vision of the family as the most natural unit gave him his vision of the family as the most supernatural unit. The only way he could secure and combine the two was to bring something new to cenobitical life. He invented the vow of stability.

From now on the brethren are supernatural brothers, supernatural sons. They are as it were begotten to the common life of monasticism by the training given to them at the hands of their common father. He in his turn must be ever conscious of his paternity, ever awake to opportunity and responsibility alike.

From this it follows that in the monastic orders the novices are normally trained at home, in the house which they have joined, and not in a common novitiate. The newest arrivals in a family are not farmed out to other families for their early formation: they must grow up in the spirit peculiar to their own household.

In the same way it is suitable that the sick and aged should be cared for, if this is possible, in the monastery of their profession. If a natural family is expected to shelter its infirm under its own roof, a religious family should be not less willing.

But the analogy of the family, if pressed too far, is apt to give too much weight to the natural and not enough to the supernatural. Unless the household is run on supernatural lines the family idea is useless.

It is exactly to guard against any sort of secularization of the life that St Benedict makes so much of the spiritual relationship existing between brother and brother, between brethren and abbot. The use of the full religious name is to remind the brethren that the natural family has been superseded. St Benedict's regulations with regard to letters and presents again show that not on all points does monastic practice take its social lead from the natural family. So also in the porter's *Deo gratias* when answering the monastery door to a guest: the phrase is not a secular formula as might be used by one secular to another, but a religious greeting as from a servant of God to a representative of Christ.

The supernatural idea is one that grows. Neither in a community nor in a soul does spirituality take shape all at once. Just as the soul draws from the community, so the community draws from traditional monasticism: the findings are pooled and out of it emerges eventually a spirit characteristic of the house.

The holiness and power of the community are measured by the degree to which this characteristic spirit is of God and unmixed with worldliness. Where there is a spirit of the world, the influence *on* the world is proportionately reduced. Where the spirit of the world dominates, neither holiness nor power can be expected to survive.

Perfection, then, personal and common, is the supreme and sole justification of the religious life. It alone verifies the vision of the founder, it is the specific contribution which religious make towards the welfare of mankind.

The common perfection of a community is moreover the only sure guarantee of divine support. For manpower as for money God makes Himself responsible, but only where He finds the serious search after holiness.

Men and women in the world are drawn towards particular religious communities, not because of the propaganda that has been launched from those houses, but because of the perfection with which the life is being lived in those houses. Even if the life is not seen from outside, the fact that it is being lived is itself a means of grace to souls. Men and women do not join a community because of the brilliance of its members, but because of the lives they lead. Perfection is the attraction. Perfection is the inspiring and exciting force.

Consequently, for a monk to isolate himself from the current of life in the community in pursuit of his own perfection is the most impeding thing he can do: it delays the perfection of the whole, and insulates him from an influence which may not be perfect but is at least more perfect than the act which severs him from the brethren.

For the monk who follows the Rule of St Benedict, the only safe perfection is cenobitic perfection. St Benedict admires the hermit life, and points the way to it for those few who have the vocation, but he does not legislate for it.

The monk who uses his monastery as a shelter within which he can erect his hermit's hut without having to bother himself about questions of self-support is deluding himself.

The monk who uses his monastic enclosure as the acreage within which he can pursue devotions undisturbed and unrelated to the devotions of others might just as well be using it as a grouse moor. The place of his profession is not a property, it is a part of him.

Thus, from the fund of spiritual vitality inherent in the body, each cell derives a vitality of its own which, by exercising rightly, it gives back again to the body. This is the law of circulation. Then out from the body into a new element goes a new vitality, imparting and inviting new life.

Whether this energy finds direction and fulfilment in making foundations, converting souls, furthering vocations, or in the indirect apostolate, unseen in result and therefore apparently unrewarded, it will certainly never be wasted. Its generation is its own consumption. Its consumption further generates.

There can be no waste where grace is responded to. Though the response is seen only by God, the willingness to be used as a channel of grace is itself a denial of waste. It is itself a response to grace.

Souls do not need to see anything in the way of results: merit is measured by love. Love is measured by love.

The only results that can be taken as guides are negative results—sins. Sin shows that grace has not been responded to. Sin points to waste; nothing else does.

To confuse unseen results with waste is the commonest of all spiritual mistakes. To work for visible result is the next most common mistake. Lack of faith is at the bottom of both.

If we think of holiness as the achievement of what we had proposed to ourselves when we entered religion, we are placing it no higher than the realization of our own character. We started off with a certain longing. Is it then holiness to have fought our way to its acknowledged attainment—and not holiness to have failed?

If we have been able to stick the flag in exactly where we wanted to see it, can we say, 'I have managed after all ... Lord, I have done the work Thou gavest me to do'? What if we wanted the wrong thing originally—the wrong flag or the wrong place to stick it? What if God gave us a different work to do—and we have not done it because of our interest in the work which we gave ourselves to do?

If we make sanctity consist in something attainable or not attainable with the means to hand, as something to be registered, weighed, valued, sealed up and put in a pigeonhole for reference, what is the difference between sanctity and anything else that we want to call our own?

We imagine that we are longing for all that is holiest when in fact what we are longing for is a form of self-realization. We are projecting ourselves. We have found a type which we admire and we are type-casting our own personality.

What we are really wanting is not God's love but our own success; not to live for His glory but for our ambition. If we were truly wanting only God's love, we would see it everywhere. But because we want our own idea of God's love, we do not see it everywhere. We see only a mirage, and this confuses us.

We do not take up sanctity as we would take up a new interest. About our interests we can be selective, we can follow our taste and change our direction on sudden impulse. Sanctity is God's selection. We follow His taste, direction, impulse.

God gives all, as St Augustine says, and we give all. Far from its being a culture it is, from our point of view, a labour. It is a labour, whole time and of no recognizable value, extending to every sort of prosaic circumstance, and calling for the exercise of every sort of boring quality. There is no aura of romance about true sanctity.

In the last analysis, sanctity, personal and common alike, is simply continuance in good. But there has to be this about it, that both the continuance and the good must be understood as God's.

First, continuance. 'The path of the just', says the book of Proverbs, 'goes forth as a shining light and increases even to perfect day'. Unless it continues to increase it will not reach perfect day. If the light is allowed to go out there will be nothing to show the difference between the path of the just and the path of the unjust. Perseverance is the condition of light: both the crowning light of vision and the light which shines on the way.

Second, the good that is continued. 'The just change their strength from good to better', writes De Osuna, commenting on Isaias, 'and not from good to worse like the statue of which Daniel speaks which deteriorated steadily from the head, but like the water passed over by the prophet, which rose higher as its volume increased. Such souls progress by flying or running and do not fail, for perfect men are not impeded by the active life they live on earth, though their conversation is in heaven in the contemplative life. Blessed will you be if you persevere in the exercise you have chosen and follow your vocation, not wandering to and fro and changing your mind. If you fluctuate you will be like a plant that cannot thrive because it is often transplanted. Do not be negligent or renounce what you have begun; then you will abide in your calling, as the Apostle advises, not passing from house to house but remaining in one, as our Lord bade His disciples.'

In the above text are comprised a homily on perseverance, a suggestion as to the conflict between the active and the contemplative vocation, and an instruction on stability. As already noted, these are subjects requiring close attention on the part of religious.

Sanctity then—not ours but God's—is the end of our endeavour as religious. 'I will go up to the palm tree', sings the bride in the Canticle, 'and will take hold of the fruit thereof.' Our study of conventual perfection should lead us to echo the bride's determination.

To follow up the symbolism of the palm in the Bridegroom's garden would fill pages of commentary. Here it may briefly be observed that the palm, in remaining always green, typifies constancy, stability, perseverance. In needing the company of other palm trees in a grove if it is to bear fruit, the palm stands for the perfection not of the solitary but of the cenobite life. Its ability to resist the storms of the desert lies in the depths of its roots and the suppleness of its stem: it is the symbol therefore of resistance to temptation and disturbance of spirit. To the Jews, who believed that it lived longer than all other trees, the palm became the symbol of eternity.

The will to 'go up into the palm tree and take hold of the fruit thereof' implies therefore the intention of living in the heights, in eternity. It implies living among others but living in interior solitude; living in the grove but also in the desert.

'I will take hold of the fruit thereof'—and take it boldly, knowing that I have not grown it myself. But if I am to grasp the fruit which is God's love, I must be holding nothing else in my hands. And if the fruit is to nourish me, I must forget about the taste of other foods.

'I will take hold of the fruit thereof'—even if it means spending my whole life climbing towards it. The fruit grows high off the ground so that my purpose may be tested. In sweat I must work my way up the tree. It is not by contemplation alone, particularly not by that contemplation which is a daydream in the clouds, that I shall be lifted up to the love of God. My work, as much as my prayer, is the test of my readiness to respond to love.

It is in my work as much as in my prayer that I shall find my true vocation. My vocation in Christ and in community is the fusion of work and prayer.

It is in work as much as in prayer that I shall find that serenity of soul which nothing can destroy. But just as prayer means steadfastness in trust and the willingness not to understand, so work means serious, unremitting and perhaps unrewarding, service in occupations the point of which again I may not be able to understand. In work as in prayer I submit my reason and my will. These are all I have.

> Despise me not,
> For I was swarthy once;
> Thou canst regard me now;
> Since Thou hast regarded me
> Grace and beauty hast Thou given me.

St John of the Cross amplifies this stanza by saying that God, 'now He has once looked upon it, and thereby adorned it with grace and beauty, may well look upon the soul a second time and increase its grace and beauty. That He has done so once, when the soul deserved it not and had no attractions for Him, is reason enough why He should do so again and again.'

The soul deserves nothing, has no attraction. 'But He that is mighty' can do great things to the soul: He can so fill it with Himself as to make it worthy of His love. Then can the soul magnify its Lord and rejoice in God its saviour. The destitute and hungry He enriches with good things, and the self-sufficient He sends empty away.

With the Thessalonians may we benefit by the prayer of St Paul when he asks that 'the God of peace Himself sanctify you in all things, that your whole spirit and soul and body may be preserved blameless in the coming of our Lord Jesus Christ. He is faithful who has called you, who will also bring it to effect.' It is to this that the religious vocation leads; this is conventual perfection.

About The Cenacle Press at Silverstream Priory

An apostolate of the Benedictine monastery of Silverstream Priory in Ireland, the mission of The Cenacle Press can be summed up in four words: *Quis ostendit nobis bona*—who will show us good things (Psalm 4:6)? In an age of confusion, ugliness, and sin, our aim is to show something of the Highest Good to every reader who picks up our books. More specifically, we believe that the treasury of the centuries-old Benedictine tradition and the beauty of holiness which has characterized so many of its followers through the ages has something beneficial, worthwhile, and encouraging in it for every believer.

www.cenaclepress.com

Also available from The Cenacle Press at Silverstream Priory

Robert Hugh Benson
The Friendship of Christ
Papers of a Pariah
Christ in the Church: A Volume of Religious Essays

Blessed Columba Marmion OSB
Christ the Ideal of the Monk
Christ in His Mysteries
Words of Life on the Margin of the Missal

Dom Hubert Van Zeller OSB
Sanctity in Other Words
The Mass in Other Words
The Will of God in Other Words
The Yoke of Divine Love

Dom Eugene Vandeur OSB
Hail Mary
The Holy Sacrifice of the Mass: Ladder of Sanctity

Hilaire Belloc
Essays of a Catholic
Hills and the Sea
First and Last

Therese of Lisieux
Just for Today
Secrets of Joy

www.cenaclepress.com